ARCHITECTURAL
STAINED GLASS

ARCHITECTURAL
STAINED GLASS

EDITED BY BRIAN CLARKE

Architectural Record Books, New York

McGraw-Hill Book Company
New York   St. Louis   San Francisco   Auckland   Bogotá
Düsseldorf   Johannesburg   London   Madrid   Mexico
Montreal   New Delhi   Panama   Paris   São Paulo
Singapore   Sydney   Tokyo   Toronto

ACKNOWLEDGMENTS

Great thanks are due to Liz Finch, Johannes and Edith Schreiter, Robert Sowers, John Piper, Myfanwy Evans, and especially to Martin Harrison.

The editor wishes to thank the Winston Churchill Memorial Trust without whose generous grant the research for this book would not have been possible.

The editors for this book were Sue Cymes and Patricia Markert, the production supervisor was Patricia Barnes Werner, and the designer was Elaine Golt Gongora. The book was set in Helvetica by Monotype Composition Company, and printed and bound by Halliday Lithograph
1234567890 HDHD 7865432109

PHOTO CREDITS

Dr. H. Oidtmann, pp. 123–131
Schreiter-Diedrichs, pp. 146, 148, 150–151, 152
Andy Earl, p. 168
Charles Frizzell, pp. 200–206, 219
Karlis Grants, pp. 214, 218, 219 top, 220–221
Alexandre Georges, p. 13
Cervin Robinson, p. 13
John Donat, pp. 8, 10

Published by Architectural Record,
A McGraw-Hill Publication,
1221 Avenue of the Americas,
New York, New York 10020
Library of Congress Cataloging in Publication Data
Main entry under title:
Architectural stained glass.
    Bibliography: p.
    Includes index.
    1. Glass painting and staining— History—
Addresses, essays, lectures. I. Clarke, Brian,
1953–
NK5306.A73   748.5'904   79-211
ISBN 0-07-011264-9

CONTENTS

ESSAYS

TOWARD A
NEW CONSTRUCTIVISM

BRIAN CLARKE

THE ROMANTIC RETREAT

It is the function of all works of art to challenge accepted norms and to undermine the social and cultural status quo. There is some considerable truth in Duchamp's maxim that unless a work of art shocks, it is of no value. The ability to shock has always rested in the hands of the few, while the susceptibility to shock rests decidedly with the many. This is because at least 90 percent of all people are traitors to the time in which they live, and it is one of the fundamental roles of the artist, who by definition must be a man of his times, to agitate and question the dictates to which society either blindly acquiesces or traditionally approves. The old description of the artist as "a man ahead of his time" is nonsensical. What separates the great artist from contemporaries is not that he is ahead of the times, but that they are behind him. He, with a vision of the future, is haunted by the spirit of the present, and works in the frenzied belief that unless he uncompromisingly articulates the *Zeitgeist* of his own era—the futuristic vision will never be realized. But, he also realizes that individual effort is insufficient and that "the final source of power in the artist is given by society, and that is precisely what is lacking in the modern artist, 'Uns tragt Kein Volk,' we have no sense of community, of a people for whom and with whom we work. That is the tragedy of the modern artist, and only those who are blind to their own social disunity and spiritual separateness blame the modern artist for his obscurity."[1]

However, the preoccupation with the cult of the past and allegiance to the spurious security offered by tradition continually grows. Art critics and dealers have become more important than artists; and academic pedantry and formalism have been placed in jurisdiction over originality and daring. Pratella's appeal in 1910 to the young artists of Italy is as pertinent now as it was then:

"I appeal to the young. Only they should listen, and only they can

Left: James Stirling: Florey Building, Queen's College, Oxford, 1966

understand what I have to say. Some people are born old, slobbering spectres of the past, cryptograms swollen with poison. To them no words or ideas, but a single injunction: the end."[2]

Manifestations of the romantic revival occur in all branches of the arts. In architecture it is the European preoccupation with conservationist, vernacular design at the expense of investigative research and discovery, the cop-out polemic of the so-called post-modernists involved, as Ada Louise Huxtable pointed out, in "quixotic aesthetic intelligence rather than art".[3] In painting, the escape into the castle-building historicist fairyland by the Brotherhood of Ruralists represents the culmination of the retreat by British artists since the late '60s into a utopian cloud–cuckoo land; a retreat that was encouraged by the British school of sloppy inadequate realists boasting among their number Hockney, Procktor, Jones, and latterly Kitaj. A parallel can be drawn in contemporary American and European photography with the followers of Edward Weston propagating a philosophy of West Coast Mysticism.[4] Fortunately however, the flight back to 1850 is not the

TOWARD A NEW CONSTRUCTIVISM

James Stirling and James Gowan:
Leicester University Engineering Building, 1959

whole story and, as in architecture, Stirling, Rogers, Pelli, and Foster attempt to come to terms with high technology and distinguish themselves above the architectural mediocrity of the '70s; and in painting, Schreiter, Motherwell, and Richard Smith go at least some way toward realizing the principles of architectonic art. Nor, mercifully, do the historicists have all their own way in photography, as the emergence and recent rise to fame of Ralph Gibson[5] proves, and whose seminal series of works, *Quadrants,* marks a turning point in the history of photography. This, along with the great achievements of Richard Rogers in architecture, Kraftwerk in music, and Schreiter in painting point toward a new constructivism.

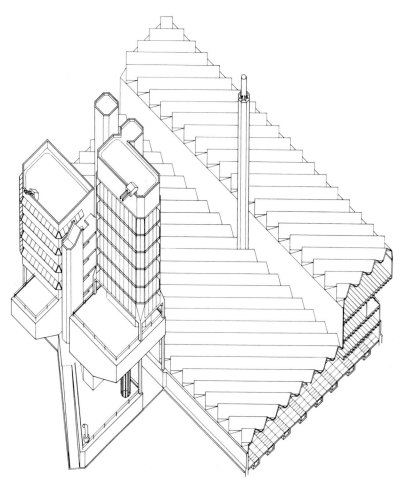

James Stirling and James Gowan:
Leicester University Engineering Building, 1959 (Axonometric)

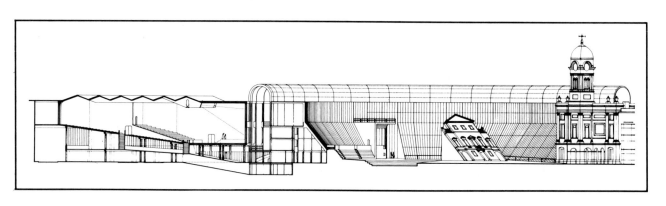

Derby Civic Centre, 1970

Foster Associates: Willis, Faber, Dumas Insurance Offices, Ipswich, 1973
Top: By day, *Bottom:* By night

Robert Motherwell:
''Elegy to the Spanish Republic XXXIV'', 1954
Albright-Knox Art Gallery, Buffalo, New York, Gift of Seymour H. Knox

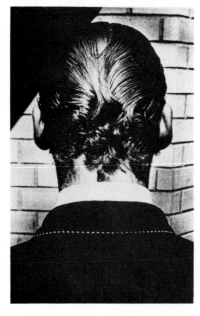 

Ralph Gibson:
From ''Days at Sea,'' 1974   From ''Quadrants,'' 1974

Richard Smith: "The Hero," 1976
(3 panels: 150 × 150 cm., 125 × 125 cm.,
100 × 100 cm.)   Collection of the Artist

Richard Smith: "Sleight of Hand," 1978
(each panel 100 × 300 cm.)

THE NEW WAVE

Since 1965, when Peter climbed out of Nick's pool[6] and Yoko Ono invited Marcel Duchamp to draw a circle,[7] the great names of the '60s innovative art have tended to go into semiretirement. Relaxing into the comfortable role of fabricators of predictable visual formulae, they have become unthreatening caricatures of their former selves. Peter Blake, who could arguably be described as the first pop artist, now paints fairies at the bottom of his garden. Allen Jones continues to paint the same woman's leg, once shocking, now prudish. Hockney, no longer even an adequate draftsman turns, by way of Picasso pastiche, to the superficial interpretation of Wallace Stevens.[8]

Foster Associates: Sainsbury Arts Centre,
University of East Anglia, 1975–78

Exactly the same situation occurred in music, and by the mid '70s, the musicians who ten years earlier had been singing along to Bob Dylan's cries for freedom were as heavily involved in the commercial structure of capitalist enterprise as the corporate figures they claimed to loathe. By 1977 and the advent of punk rock and the New Wave, the situation in rock music had regressed to a point of almost total rhetorical self-indulgence. There was for the now established musicians no longer any cause to fight or angry fist to be shaken now that they had wealth and the ability to manipulate. The arrival of a New-Wave music represented a total rejection of "middle class" rock 'n roll and an equally vehement rejection of the life style personified by the aging stars of American and British pop. Punk rock, however, brought with it a great deal more than a reshuffling of stardom. It articulated the vitriolic disapproval by the young of the sneaking complacency in music, art, politics, and perhaps most important of all—the environment. Life had become too self-assured; there was no longer any threat, any challenge or visual impetus to encourage individual creative expression—only repetitive formulae. It is no coincidence that between the autumn of 1976 and the summer of 1977, a period in which the New Wave was at its most intense and outrageous, many prominent bands adopted names expressing their awareness of the standard of life they were expected to lead, *High Rise Living, Suburban Studs, Subway Sect.* None of the pop stars who supposedly represented them sang about unemployment, about satellite towns, or inadequate schools and teachers. The only music they knew was spineless commercial cliches posing as "heavy" rock 'n roll.

Architecture meant the government housing developments which on every level were grossly incompetent and patronizing. Art was the gilt-framed old masters, with Hockneys and Warhols owned by the people who inhabited glossy ads. Threatened by the suffocation of median respectability, they totally abandoned the codes and morals of a failed generation, exposing the inconsequential narcissism of the Superstar, rejecting the ever-increasing pressure from architects, musicians, politicians, etc., to become the "blank generation." At this point, the mantle of avant-gardism passed from the shoulders of the artists and art students to the punks and there it stays, only occasionally being worn by one who spans both worlds.

The New Wave, like the futurists, adopted the by-now world-famous symbols of violence and aggression. Body art, for so long the undefiled area of the elitist artistic cognoscenti, became common knowl-

Page from *Steve's Paper* Punk-rock Fanzine, 1977

edge and went out of the art gallery into the street. It was the most positive creative expression of autonomy of the twentieth century. "Leave your job—buy a guitar." And those least likely to heed this primal cry or appreciate its significance were the countless artists to whom urban life and high technology were symbols of a time in which they would rather not have been born. They, the respectable architects, distinguished artists, and socialist politicians, were directly responsible in preparing the right ground for punk rock.

THE COLLABORATIVE PRINCIPLE
Art and Architecture

As punk rock was able to sweep the board clean and make room for new constructive expression in music, so must the board be cleared in visual art; and it is somewhere between the disciplines of art and architecture that the "new constructivism" will be conceived. The self-inflicted isolation of the contemporary artist and the mistrust often leveled against the architect are both important contributing factors in the current situation of architectural art. The painter is anxious to keep intact the historical image of artist as loner, the intense sensitive, the genius and "maestro"; while the architect, feeling the watchful eye of his client constantly over his shoulder, approaches any extra-to-budget expense, such as art, with considerable trepidation, guarding jealously any intrusion into *his* building by potential glory-thieves. However, in fairness to the architect (in this instance, architects as opposed to builders with architectural degrees), it must be stated that he has not, in the past fifty years, seen much evidence of the successful marriage of art to architecture, nor indeed has there been much room in the modernist post-Miesian aesthetic for the introduction of arbitrary nonfunctional elements. Sadly, the heights to which the average architect is able to aspire in his sanctioning of the principles of architectonic art is the introduction into his building of the occasional "decorative wall feature," usually mounted above the "decorative foliage feature." But what proof has the open-minded architect that the inclusion of art into contemporary, modernist or even post-modernist building has ever been successful? It is likely that he will recall the Chagall mural in Harrison and Abramovitz's Metropolitan Opera House[9] or Sutherland's tapestry in Spence's Coventry Cathedral, or one of the countless mosaics or sculptures in any one of thousands of urban shopping precincts throughout Europe and the USA. What is very unlikely is that he will think of the Albers in the Architects

Left: Kasimir Malevitch: Suprematist Painting, 1915
Right: Kasimir Malevitch: Suprematist Painting, c. 1920

Collaborative's Pan Am Building[10] or Calder's stabiles[11] in Lincoln Center, Kennedy Airport, or UNESCO Paris, and Saché, or of the Schreiter in Leutesdorf, the Meistermann at Bottrop, or, what must be one of the greatest amalgamations of art and architecture—Noguchi's tilted red cube set directly in front of Skidmore Owings and Merrill's 140 Broadway. The existing examples of works of art designed as a result of the collaborative principle are miniscule.

THE COMPLETE BUILDING

"The complete building is the final aim of the visual arts. Their noblest function was once the decoration of buildings. Today they exist in isolation, from which they can be rescued only through the conscious, cooperative effort of all craftsmen. Architects, painters, and sculptors must recognize anew the composite character of a building as an entity. Only then will their work be imbued with the architectonic spirit which it has lost as a 'salon art.'

Architects, sculptors, painters, we must all turn to the crafts.

Art is not a profession. There is no essential difference between the

Mies van der Rohe:
Collage Study: Music Room as Architectural Problem
& Its Relationship to Sculpture, c. 1940

artist and the craftsman. In rare moments of inspiration, moments beyond the control of his will, the grace of heaven may cause his work to blossom into art. But proficiency in his craft is essential to every artist. Therein lies a source of creative imagination. Let us create a new guild of craftsmen, without the class distinctions which raise an arrogant barrier between craftsman and artist. Together let us conceive and create the new building of the future, which will embrace architecture and sculpture and painting in one unity and which will rise one day towards heaven from the hands of a million workers like the crystal symbol of a new faith."[12]

Four years prior to Gropius' proclamation of the first Bauhaus, Vladimir Mayakovsky had demanded proletariat art and the end of the salon tradition:

Skidmore Owings Merrill
140 Broadway, 1967
''Red Cube'' by Noguchi

Mies van der Rohe and Philip Johnson:
House of Seagram, 1958

"We do not need a dead mausoleum of art where dead works are worshipped, but a living factory of the human spirit—in the streets, in the tramways, in the factories, workshops and workers' homes."[13]

Both Mayakovsky and Gropius were, in fact, seeking the same end—the unconditional destruction of the salon tradition, removing art from the gallery to the public place; in short they wanted what Léger called "Art on public display . . ." and an end to "bourgeois art privately owned and viewed in dead museums."[14]

Photography had long since freed painters from the suffocating restrictions of pure imitation and the time was right for visual artists to look beyond the painted canvas for means of expression. At first, photography was the obvious solution, but few painters were brave enough to risk forgoing "real art" for the photographic image.[15] It is only today that photography, on a large scale, has come to be accepted as a totally valid art form despite the work of Emerson, Nadar, Cartier–Bresson, Sander, and others, as well as Duchamp who, in 1922, wrote to Stieglitz, "You know exactly how I feel about photography. I would like to see it make people despise painting until something else will make photography unbearable."[16] Duchamp applauded the new generation of photographers because they laughed in the face of elite art and attacked sacrosanct aesthetic barriers. They were as much disciples of the machine age as Léger, El Lissitsky, Malevitch or Mies, daring to use such a mechanized object as the camera for the production of art. But photography only answered some of the problems posed by the "art object," and far from destroying the myth of the precious art object, by rejecting the gallery system and relying entirely upon its reproductive properties for the dissemination of photographic information, photography has become part of the system that fifty years ago it seriously questioned.[17]

Thus, even for performing artists and photographers, galleries and museums remain the source or the major part of their income, and in many cases the singular end and goal to which they aspire. But if, in fact, the very dubious commercial gallery and equally worrying museum system are the heights of achievement, then visual art as such must by definition be dead. However, life passes into it as soon as visual art leaves the museum or gallery doorway and approaches the factory and office-block. At this stage, the collaborative principle between architect as coordinator and artist as designer must begin. As previously mentioned, the collaborative idea is viewed with considerable mistrust by both architect and artist alike, usually on the grounds that collaboration is synonymous with compromise. But art, like architecture, can only be major when it is totally uncompromising, when the artist refuses to be influenced by the pressures of his patron to make his work respectable, unobjectionable—hence mediocre—when he refuses to make these suggested "minor additions" on the grounds that any addition to the truth detracts from it.

Such concessions are impossible for the serious artist in the same way that they are inconceivable to the serious architect. The architect's problems in commissioning artists are usually financial. According to Vitruvius, the three classic conditions of good building are commodity, firmness, and delight. Today we have much experience of the first two qualities, architects being able to plan with economy and convenience and sound building techniques; yet, we have little evidence of the third condition, delight, being met. Indeed, before he can lift bland, lifeless buildings out of the utilitarian rut enforced by an inflationary economy, the architect often is dependent on the generosity of the public and donations from the federal arts organizations, and this is usually after the building's completion. When such a situation occurs, the artist acts as the cosmetic surgeon carrying out what beauticians would call "remedial camouflage." As Venturi pointed out in 1966, "Industry promotes expensive industrial and electronic research, but not architectural experiments, and the federal government diverts subsidies toward air transportation, communication, and the vast enterprises of war, or, as they call it, national security, rather than toward the forces for the direct enhancement of life. The practicing architect must admit this. In simple terms, the budgets, techniques, and programs for his buildings must relate more to 1866 than 1966."[18]

On this level, commissioned architectural art is frequently arbitrary and singular, working on a monofunctional rather than a "multivalent" level, becoming servile or dictatorial to either extreme.[19] While great art can occur within the restraints of such a situation, it is only despite the circumstances—not owing to them.[20] For the building and the art to operate as one unit while fulfilling the various functions and aspirations of the architectural complex, collaboration must start at a logical point—which is the beginning. The artwork must be conceived as part of the building to the extent that, removed from an architectural context, it would lose a great deal, if not all, of its strength. Collaboration at its highest level is when the artist ceases to be a decorator and becomes, alongside the architect, a joint manipulator of architectural space, working towards a single if not composite goal.

ART AND FUNCTION
Polychromatic Architecture

Richard Rogers, in his account of design decisions he and Renzo Piano employed when working on the Centre Pompidou says, "we have always consciously designed with color because of our interest in what Renzo and I call happy buildings, buildings that people react to. In the Centre Beaubourg we adopted the British Standard code for industrial colors (used for marking hazards and identifying certain equipment) as a basic direction to follow; the significance being that we are seeking rules so that our color decisions do not stem from arbitrary preferences. We begin color selection, therefore, with a process of elimination through color coding."[21]

Unfortunately, Piano's and Rogers' view of the integrated use of color as expressed in the Centre Pompidou is not commonly shared, and frequently we find color used arbitrarily to disguise the inadequacies of the architect—who fondly imagines that by introducing a "capricious element" in the form of applied external color, he is also glossing over the omnipresent fact that his buildings are grossly incompetent. A blue door here and a yellow one there are not enough to distract the inhabitants of speculatively built housing estates from seeing their homes as patronizing and leveling. To quote Léger:

"Architecture is surface and volume. The qualities of volume are inherent; with surface they are relative, living or dead.

"Man, set on living in an architectural environment, demands a reasonable quality of both dead and living surfaces.

"Architectural surface is either the horizontal or the vertical plane and is defined by volume.

"What then takes place? A balance of the need, if any, of the architect and his client to 'decorate'. Most men obey the 'decorative' instinct under the pressure of 'horror vacui'. This 'horror vacui' makes use of the 'decorative' quality to negate itself by means of the living or dead surface. The 'decorative' quality takes the form of colour and the object itself: the attributes are there and they can be used.

"Architecture is organisation directed towards a rational and beautiful solution of all these values. Today this is a pressing problem and it is considered by active groups of modern artists the whole world over, and especially during the last few years.

"In every case their effort and achievement is considerable. Modern artists want to rank the various qualities, they want to re-establish the principle of a plastic hierarchy.

Foster Associates: Electronics Factory, Wiltshire, 1966

''The struggle is sharpest between the manufactured object and the art object (a picture, a relief) and the desire of modern architects to absorb them by their reduction to no more than a means of action in an organised ensemble.

''Surface colour (a decorative quality) must be used with rigorous discernment to be a natural function of architecture.

''In order to create a calm and anti-dynamic atmosphere, a plastic order in colour inside or outside, certain knowledge of the relevant values are needed.

''Pure colour must be viable for internal and external application to maximize its value: thus a square metre of yellow dominates an area four times its size. Replace it with a piece of red furniture and it too would by power of expansion dominate a considerable area.

''The dynamic quality (picture or object) does have the right to a place in this organization. Man is instinctively attracted by the movement created by an object like a child with something shiny. As for colours, the crux is in the quantity. Colour and the object have their plastic rationale: to facilitate a calm ensemble where the place for the sharp and unexpected is filled by the people who happen to be there.

"In this new environment a man can be seen, for the eye is not distracted by dispersed qualities. Everything is arranged. Against these big calm areas the human face assumes its proper status. A nose, eye, foot, hand or jacket button will become a precise reality. The concept of an intelligent hierarchy of plastic possibilities is extremely modern and constitutes objective realism at its most powerful."[22]

Since 1945 there has been a corporate architectural rejection of the use of color, and the morality of *beton-brut* has almost totally overpowered the influences of Theo van Doesburg, Mondrian, Léger, and Le Corbusier. But the re-emergence of interest in applied color coincides with the new popularity of the nineteenth-century polychrome architects Butterfield, Burges, Pearson, Ricardo, and the structure painter of our own time, Chermayeff.

THE WINDOW

The aesthetic positive use of standard-colored building materials and components, such as orchestrated by Piano and Rogers at the Centre Pompidou and by Norman Foster at the Sainsbury Centre and Design Research Unit at Ryegate, houses the same spirit that has motivated a small though important number of artists, who since 1945, have been designing so-called stained glass. One of such, Jochem Poensgen, recalls: "Even as a boy I always felt strongly attracted to art on public display; the open inclusion of painting and sculpture in architecture in the history of art seemed to me evidence of a 'golden age.' The optimistic utterances of Fernand Léger about the possibilities of 'Art on public display' greatly confirmed my ideas. My turning to glass art as a possible way of realizing these ideas was a logical consequence."[23]

Unlike painting, which when used architecturally is usually applied to an existing wall after the design stage; glass is a basic architectural material with essential roles of function to fulfill.

"The material history of architecture shows that through the centuries there has been a ceaseless struggle in favour of light against the obstacle imposed by the law of gravity."[24]

The history of architecture up until the nineteenth century had been concerned with load-bearing walls of brick or stone; these had been mostly in the construction of buildings of any size, giving high thermal

22

TOWARD A NEW CONSTRUCTIVISM

Foster Associates: Sainsbury Arts Centre,
University of East Anglia, 1975–78

insulation and thermal capacity with low solar admission and relatively low loss through the windows due to the constructional limitations in the wall openings.

Building technology in the nineteenth century was concerned with the development of iron, first as cast iron, then as wrought iron, and later as steel. At the end of this century, reinforced concrete appeared as the new material. The ascendancy of the lightweight framed structure began in 1796 with the iron-framed spinning mill at Ditherington, and the following forty years saw a development in factories of up to eight or nine stories with iron columns and beams, but supported by load-bearing facades.

It was not until the 1860s that the post and lintel showed itself on the facade to support infill panels of brick and glass. This structural expression was first seen not in the United States, but the contemporary Oriel Chambers (1864), Liverpool, is a typical example from the United Kingdom. The development of steel in the 1890s opened the way for the large multistory building, and the possibility of framed construction caught designers' imaginations in terms of the skyscraper.

At about this time, flat glass manufacturing techniques developed sufficiently to produce large panes of glass adequate to infill the frame construction. Glass, therefore, became the inevitable material for the lightweight facade. To further lighten the facade, the curtain wall of the 1930s was a logical development of the metal window technique after the invention of the metal extrusion of the 1890s. The Peter Jones store of Sloane Square, London, was, in 1935, one of the first; while in the United States, Lever House in New York (1952) was the paragon of the air-conditioned curtain-wall office.

Recent developments in glass technology have allowed glass to be used as a structural support, enabling large openings to be enclosed by an all-glass system. This, then, is the most recent structural development in window technology towards what Le Corbusier calls "the struggle for light."

The principal functions of window glass are concerned with the view out (and sometimes the view in) and the internal visual amenity in terms of daylight for task illumination and for quality illumination.

Structural and environmental developments in glass technology have produced visual qualities in the glazing which are entirely incidental to its technical performance. Visual qualities of form, color, reflection, and transmission in the glass cause the character of the building to change as the prevailing lighting conditions change during the day.[25]

The development of the extended use of flat glass in architecture comes some way toward the realization of Paul Scheerbart's *Glasarchitektur,* published in 1914, and of which Reyner Banham said, "of all the visionary writings of that period this book has the greatest impact nowadays as the concrete and tangible vision of the future environment of man."[26] From "Environment and Its Influence on the Development of Culture"[27] Scheerbart says, "we live for the most part in closed rooms. These form the environment from which our culture grows. Our culture is to a certain extent the product of our architecture. If we want our culture to rise to a higher level, we are obliged, for better or for worse, to change our architecture. And this only becomes possible if we take away the closed character from the rooms in which we live. We can only do that by introducing glass architecture, which lets in the light of the sun, the moon, and the stars, not merely through a few windows but through every possible wall, which will be made entirely of glass—of coloured glass. The new environment which we thus create, must bring a new culture."

The expression of this new culture has certainly begun, if not a little late, and owing very little to the artists throughout Europe and the USA who have claimed to be committed to the use of stained glass in architecture. One wonders why this is so when looking at the windows designed by Albers in 1922–23, van Doesburg in 1923–27, and Thorn Prikker in 1931–39. The main reason for this is the craft-art dichotomy.

THE NEW CONSTRUCTIVISM

The modern history of stained glass is the history of a minor art, minor because, since the retinal revolution of the 19th century, the number of important investigative works in stained glass is minute. This is largely the result of the anachronistic purism of a host of stained-glass craftsmen who guard jealously the "all my own work" myth. This myth still finds expression today in the critical attack made by pensioner glass stainers on the post-war school of German designers who have their windows fabricated by firms of technicians. The artist-studio relationship that has existed in Germany since the 1920s is unique and has, among other things, played a major part in making West Germany the home of the most important school of stained-glass artists in history. This, doubled with the building legislation of the post-war federal republic promoting the inclusion of art in all building projects and the favorable tax concessions to patrons, not to mention the vast rebuilding of Germany in the aftermath of the defeat, has produced a climate perfect for the development of architectural art. However, because so much new church building was going on, now largely completed, artists working in stained glass were inundated with ecclesiastical commissions and found no need to pursue, nor presumably felt any commitment to, a secular employment of the medium. Consequently, even in Germany, stained glass goes through a recession period and heads towards a worrying return to the semirealist aesthetic of pre-war Europe. In the last few years it has also become increasingly apparent that only a few of the many German artists who have achieved fame since the 1950s have produced work that ranks alongside the achievements of the same period in German painting, film-making, and architecture. This is largely because they, like so many English and American stained-glass designers, have become specialists—designing only stained glass and mosaics and restricting their terms of reference and vocabulary to an essentially limited media. Such specialization is as dangerous in stained glass as in painting, if not more.

The new constructivism in art, which seeks to manifest itself in all media, is by nature broad and versatile, requiring an equal versatility in artists' terms of reference. The days of the art specialist are over, and the multidisciplinary mind of the new constructivists spans all disciplines in the pursuit of the realization of the collaborative principle.

A SHORT HISTORY OF THE DEVELOPMENT OF TWENTIETH-CENTURY GERMAN STAINED GLASS

M. COULON–RIGAUD

Even in Germany, the conscious decision to free stained glass from the academic approach of the *fin de siécle* stemmed from art nouveau. The work of Emile Bernard (1868–1941), with its orientation toward two-dimensional, arabesque art in which a few glowing colors are constrained and intensified by dark oscillating contours, inspired by medieval glass art, caused the French art critics to speak of *cloisonisme.* In fact, his work is sometimes reminiscent of stained-glass cartoons.

This flat visual concept, with its graphic rhythmical style lacking the central perspective of illusionism—which even Cézanne helped to destroy in the last quarter of the nineteenth century in order to reintroduce a visual structure—finally helped the pioneers of the Jugendstijl movement to discover the ideal presuppositions for a new approach in glass art. In Germany, this primarily involved Peter Behrens (1868–1940), Hans Christiansen (1866–1945), Walter Leistikow (1865–1908), and Adolf Hoelzel (1853–1934).[1]

It is generally acknowledged that widely diverse ideas and influences—artistic, sociopolitical, religious (theosophical or deistic) and philosophical—were responsible for the worldwide onset of art nouveau. This is made manifest in many works of artistic, social, and cultural pertinence. Reactions against the cultural poverty of the nineteenth century appear conspicuously anti-academic and individualistic. The artist rediscovered his subjectivity to life and not doctrines and became concerned with expressing all aspects of reality.

Their refusal to sacrifice fervent individual claims of originality to the desire for integration is what fundamentally differentiates the expressionist stained-glass sector—the Max Pechsteins (1881–1955), César Kleins (1876–1954), Ewald Dülbergs (1888–1933) and Karl Schmidt-Rottluffs (1884–1976)—from the more or less contemporary protagonists of Jugendstijl. An example of this is the small bust of

Christ which Schmidt-Rottluff carved in 1919, treating natural material in a distinctly aethiopic manner. As in Nolde's work, the color tone is bawled out in an emotional state rather than sung.

In this tense atmosphere of mythical perplexity, optimism, tolerance of un-Christian ideas, and a cynical approach to society, the Dutchman Johan Thorn Prikker achieved the initial breakthrough which set the scene for the development of stained glass to this day. Exposing himself wholeheartedly to numerous influences led him to self-discovery rather than eclecticism. The more important of these influences were: the theories of the Pre-Raphaelites; the profound diversity of French symbolism; the theosophy of Sâr Peladan; his friendship with van de Velde; contact with Toulouse-Lautrec and poets such as Maeterlinck, Verhaeren, or Verlaine; and his links with both the group of expressionists formed around Gottfried Heinersdorff in Berlin, with whom he travelled to Chartres in 1913, and the mystical philosophies of the *Blaue Reiter.* Further influences were his early experiences of Asiatic and Egyptian art and the revolutionary views of the cubists, particularly the Orphists. Thorn Prikker's key work, the ten large windows in the chancel and main passageways of the Church of the Three Queens in Neuss, was designed in 1911–12. Following Thorn Prikker's work up to 1930, it is evident that his primary aim was to free pictorial art from the dregs of its decline.[2] The symbolism of content and the realism of the environment are separated further by structures which become purer and purer.

His statement in 1920 that one should avoid any kind of figurative content explains the gradual transformation of his visual conception, which brings him closer and closer to the purist guidelines of the De Stijl group, founded in 1917. By the end of the '20s and the beginning of the '30s, there were hardly any diagonal movements in his windows, in keeping with the aesthetic concept of the De Stijl movement, i.e., the subjugation of form to the basic perpendicular and horizontal elements. This was one of the primary disciplines of abstraction demanded by Mondrian as the "denaturalizing" effect of the work of art, the aim being mastery of matter.

Josef Albers (1888–1976), during his Dessau period, had the initiative to bring Paul Klee's drawing, *The Cathedral Windows of Our Century,* produced when he was Master of Form at the Bauhaus, right into line with the axioms of the De Stijl ideology, and to realize Klee's first offering in glass designs of strict prosody. If there is a Bauhaus style of stained glass, then Albers essentially typified it in 1921 and 1922 with his numerous screen windows, e.g., the windows in the Sommerfeld House in Berlin, built by Walter Gropius. Similar experiments were made by Theo van Doesburg (1883–1931) and Sophie Taueber-Arp (1889–1943).

The German stained-glass scene of the '30s, '40s, and early '50s was chiefly dominated by two personalities: Heinrich Campendonk (1889–1957)[3] and Anton Wendling (1891–1965). Both were pupils of Thorn Prikker and both extended their achievements in their own way. Campendonk became a member of the *Blaue Reiter* in 1911, and in his search for a decorative harmony in figurative art, reabsorbed the initiatives of cubism with just as much gusto as those professing the *neue sachlichkeit.* Wendling took his ascetic language of shapes primarily from the late ungraphic phase of Thorn Prikker. In rejecting the vehement asymmetry of De Stijl, Wendling reduced the figurative element to ornament, thus giving it a flexible rapport. This overall declaration produced by the mass repetition of ornamental motifs remained a one-off example in twentieth-century stained glass.[4]

After the Second World War, German glass reached a height unequalled since the middle ages—distinguished by its modernity and clarity. Though various logical reasons can be found for this success, it remains an unaccountable phenomenon in a generation that has been forcibly cut off from contemporary cultural events for twelve years—while living in a climate of religious fixation for the proven and assured. Yet, the few artists who attempted to innovate found open eyes and ears.

Let us begin with Georg Meistermann (b. 1911) who, owing to the wide range of art-historical labels one could attach to him, is as difficult to assess as his artistic origins. Though a pupil of Heinrich Mauen and Ewald Matare, his early windows demonstrate an active disagreement with the artistic stance of Thorn Prikker.[5] He declines from the start to make use of any ornament which is even remotely reminiscent of geometry or pattern, however appropriate this possibility might be. Everything in his work has movement—there is no use of the object as sum total of perfectly calculated form. Konrad Pfaff's slightly contrived, but nevertheless justifiable, notion of a "new ataraxy"[6] in describing Schaffrath's work would be completely inapplicable to the spontaneity and disturbance in Meistermann's windows. His work encompasses not only the generally uneasy combinations of figures, symbols, and absolute visual vocabulary, but also a rich, vibrant use of color and an inexhaustible repertoire of symbols.[7]

It is indeed true that modern glass art, as Meistermann once said, evolved from Tafelmalerei—that is clear from his own work—as well as that of Manessier, Léger, Rouault, and Schreiter. But the pictorial and graphic works of Meistermann and Schreiter offer much more than a few monumental examples. The whole spectrum of German post-war art was widened by such glass images, introducing aspects which are simply unrealizable on canvas. That is precisely why, for example, Meistermann's *Bottrop Spiral* (1958), which gave momentum to his generation well into the '60s, is undeniably a milestone in the history of abstract pictorial semantics; and Schreiter's *Explosion in Burgstadt* (1960)[8] is a shining example of the outgoing German informal period, with which only the prolific scattering of light in his *Heilig Geist* windows in Bremen Neue-Vahr (1964) bears comparison. It is clear from his windows in St. Clemens in Mayen (1973) the profundity Meistermann is capable of achieving when it comes to the intensification of color tones. The stir caused by his early windows (e.g., in Cologne broadcasting studios, the Cathedral Sepulchre of Würzburg, and in St. Kilians, Schweinfurt) because of their marked innovative features had the most lasting effect on those who also were seeking new directions; and even among those who were producing comparably independent work, there is hardly one who could deny the impact of Meistermann's richly developed ideas on their work. One cannot overlook the fact that the impulses which began with him were especially fruitful and effective in the Rhineland. The fact that such initial sparks don't necessarily have to determine the style of those who kindle them is clearly seen in the development of Jochem Poensgen's work (b. 1931)[9], and in the noticeably less smooth development of the versatile and gifted Joachim Klos (b. 1931).[10]

The very diverse schools of objective glass art were practically unaffected by the impact of this breakthrough into the unknown. Apart from Campendonk's pupil, Wilhelm Teuwen (1908–1976), whose bizarre whims are manifested surreally in individualistic and graceful images, hardly any of the graphic glass artists, even in France, deserted the well-trodden path. Neo-expressionists in stained glass after 1945, highly praised and patronized by conservative circles, stagnated visibly as a result of the noncritical complacency of their advocates.

A similar thing happened to the wide phalanx of Bauhaus adherents who were concerned ultimately with the final products, supposedly refined to the last detail, and with things devoid of application, such as standardized units. The resulting inoffensiveness of form caused the basic constructivist stance of the last two decades to degenerate into a commercial bourgeois aesthetic. One cannot say that every work by Emil Kiess (b. 1930) or Helmut Lander (b. 1924) escapes this condemnation either.

In my opinion, the outstanding facet in the achievement of Ludwig Schaffrath (b. 1944) is that he explored characteristics of the art form formulated by the Bauhaus and practiced during the '50s by industry, and by 1960 had evolved a highly personal visual language.[11] Indeed, Meistermann's "special designs," in which three-dimensional perspective gives the structure depth and substance, also play an important part in Schaffrath's windows, in a rationalized form. His walls of glass, with their emphasis on order, are generally architectonic in that they create a visual effect out of the unlikely starting point of something which essentially has a structural purpose. Even the lack of sequence in Schaffrath's windows proves to be an element of harmony in the building; in fact, this helps to define a new sense of order by illustrating the incompleteness of what seemed to be a perfect structure. Consequently, their function is not to cause visual discord, but to render human the concept of order. Schaffrath shows the same sort of belief in this conscious "neutralization" of discrepancies and potential breaches as does Schreiter in the formal intensification of conflicts.

Johannes Schreiter (b. 1930), whose whole work stems from duality as a basic condition of existence, has developed for this ambiguous world a visual language which cannot be misinterpreted. Vast, serene "stationary walls," or geometrical structures, represent rationality, timelessness, survival—the unwielding hard core in contrast to emotion and decay. This dialectic, still apparent between the architectural and visual in his glass walls at Leutesdorf, is evident in his stained glass after 1965 in that the tensions produced by the medium must be contained by the disciplines of physical space. Thus, Schreiter's concept of integration is no longer successfully achieved by assimilation of the visual into the heart of the architectural, but more by playing down the contradictions through an emphasis on understated relationships between space and image.

In experiencing such environments, the aesthetic pleasure, thus held back to a certain extent, is free from distractions; for here occurs what literary historian Friedrich once described as the "transformation of the perceptible into the unfamiliar," with reference to Mallarmé.

Schreiter's special contribution to contemporary glass art lies primarily in his liberation of the medium through exploration of lead as a graphic and autonomous theme.[12] Hence, the design element in his windows is pure and inexhaustibly diverse. It wanders across monochromatic color areas and, when necessary, leaves behind disruptions in the apparently inviolable constructions of lattices, or areas for meditation. Recently, since 1974, Schreiter disturbs the stability of his laconic visual construction in a different way. Narrow tendril-like trimmings, or at least sections of them, which have an enclosing function, suddenly break off and, taking up the neurotic, sinewy rhythm of his line, fly off into "emptiness," sometimes even over the barriers of floating lattices.[13]

Since 1960, Wilhelm Buschulte (b. 1923) has been concerned with the possibilities of the organic form already utilized by Jugendstijl. Indeed, his beginnings—apart from some figurative attempts—lie in symbolism through chance stylization of geometrical scenery, which may be the reason that time and time again he turned to geometry and symmetry. But his best-known work is the organic *Fables* which, seen from certain angles, suggest growth patterns of plant forms. Once again, in my opinion, a style of working which is far from random, though it may well be inspired by subjectivity, has little in common with automatic art. The unpretentious style of Buschulte has its closest parallel in naive art. Indeed, it is too narrow a belief that in art the naive approach can only be seen in portrayal of the objective worlds. As far as I am concerned, Buschulte, when compared to Hans Ostendorf or Ludwig Schaffrath, at least in the sphere of his unburdened, sinuous, visual ornamentalism and use of color, is an abstract "naive." My theory is supported both by the fluid "cellular" sections in Essen Cathedral and the separating and multiplying of amoeboid, coagulated shapes in his windows at the Chapel of St. Catherine's Hospital at Unna (1968).

The fact that Buschulte did not allow his tapestries, the last of which are close to op art (but long since pledged to pure geometry), to follow his organic intentions, but instead worked simultaneously at both treatments, is, firstly, a proof of his versatility; and, secondly, an argument in favor of the theory that "reason of conception" is not a term compatible with a less constrained, i.e., more naive, relationship with art.[14]

In conclusion is one more observation on the German stained-glass panorama, which I have surveyed for at least twenty years, and for which I owe most profuse thanks to Johannes Schreiter: it is, regrettably, impossible to produce a like-minded progeny, except in the case of a few relatively well-matured offspring, which therefore makes the influence which those mentioned have already had on the younger generation of other countries astonishing.

THE RAW MATERIAL GLASS AS A LIGHT FILTER

JOHANNES SCHREITER

COLOR—NOT A VEHICLE FOR ESCAPING REALITY, BUT A MEDIUM FOR CONSCIOUSNESS

We haven't always had the technical, aesthetic, or spiritual requisites to realize the potential of colored light for contemplative environments. This is proved not only by the clear glass on *grisailles* of the twelfth and thirteenth centuries based on Bernhard Von Clairvaux's claims,[1] but also by the rejection of colored environments in the centuries of enlightenment and classicism.

But what is meant by the term, "colored environment?" By abandoning the objectivity of daylight, an atmospheric light remains, which by permeating the interior, alters the color and essential nature of objects within. Simultaneously, a predesigned spiritual mood is created. Thus, the visitor is helped toward, or even into, the process of self-abandonment. He leaves behind mundane realities and moves in a new sphere of mental associations and relationships with his surroundings.

Twentieth-century Western man is conditioned to this transcendentalism; not in the way that beliefs and doctrines in the middle ages pervaded all aspects of life, but in the sense that modern symbolism provides an antithetic reality, an alternative to the demands of everyday life. Since the nineteenth century, this tension between world and anti-world, between concept and actuality, has determined the spiritual environment of Western man—embodied in visual art, literature, and music.[2]

The last fifteen years have seen the decline of color as preprogramming for man and environment—this deserves our attention. Let us look away from the reactionary approach behind various movements of contemporary art, which are concerned with rectifying, destroying, or distancing oneself from the predominantly aesthetic past.[3] Also, let us ignore the notorious predilection for strictness that such reactionaries find their only justification. We are left, then, with the unmistakable tendency to render the celebration of communion in the Church more acceptable through the medium of art, and there is no doubt at all that Bultmann and his school's efforts at demythologizing play a fundamental role in this exoneration.[4] As always, in times of change, the real agent in the background is society, whose displeasure now, as in the past, is demonstrated by the individual, and translated into a constructive form.

The mass media employs every possible means, including color, to thoughtlessly manipulate society; hence, man is on the defensive and shows an insurpassable degree of mistrust and a yearning for autonomy. It is, therefore, all too understandable that even the phenomenon of color meets with rejection and skepticism. Everyone knows that in the course of the day he is going to be deliberately enticed by color; he knows that color, which Cézanne was able to define as the surface expression of profundity, rising up from the roots of the earth, is today one of the fallen angels of consumer demagogy.

Likewise, we cannot overlook the glassy concrete expanses of new satellite towns, where the main use of color is to make money, and where it is abused in order to mask and distract from the dilettante functional architecture so dangerous to society. Are not such practices basically as terrible as the various reactionary cults who use color in a similar way as a vehicle for escaping reality? This attempted flight from an increasingly banal and leveling reality is indeed a thoroughly legitimate aspect of contemporary art, but only in so far as it offers standards for breaking down the undesirable elements, rather than overwhelming one.

This is certainly one reason that progressive theologists, architects, and church artists make more and more demonstrative use of harmonics, preferring an ascetic use of color in the metamorphosis of material environment and psyche. Thus, we have a rejection of the idea of an expressive image presiding over the place of worship. Images, or their basic elements, must become a tool again in the task of strengthening and developing architecture. This priority must particularly apply to windows of colorless white or gray glass. If we face a multicolored glass image, no matter how intense the artistic content is, one's attention is dominated. In the case of neutral glass, the observer remains unmolested and detached, being devoid of the transforming effects of a colored light source, his attention being drawn to specific content. Thus, *grisailles*, on one hand, lack the drug effect of color, and on the other hand, contain the stimulus to reach the consciousness of personal will power.

NO REDUCTION OF REALITY TO UNTRUTH, BUT OF UNTRUTH TO REALITY

We are up against other imponderables. Art, theology, and religion have at times taken upon themselves a pathos which, by its apodictic manifestations, sacrificed a great deal of pure feeling and "soberness of the spirit." As a reaction, we have learned to use small modest gestures to great effect. This ought to culminate in the abandonment of mental crutches, untruths, and doubts, but not further into glorification of the rational which, by its one-dimensionalism, can offer only familiar insights into man's identity. Regrettably, Susanne Langer is all too accurate in maintaining that contemporary man's highest aim is to transform fiction and belief into reality. "That's why man periodically expresses his contempt of religious or legendary tradition; his satisfaction over the naked realism in literature;" (it would be worth expanding here: in music, pictorial art, and the so-called news reporting of the mass media) "his mistrust and impatience in relation to poetry; and perhaps on the naive uncritical level of the average mentality, the passion for 'news'."[5]

I am, therefore, not speaking of reduction of reality to untruth, as continually occurs in people's perception of facts; but, of a reduction of untruth to reality—and by reduction, in the sphere of art, I am not advocating aesthetic understatement and loss of content, but that form and content undergo a process of selection. We cannot ignore the fact that alongside the process of reduction begins a gradual loss of individuality, and this inevitably poses a threat to the development of new forms, which is always vital.

One must take into consideration the fact that in today's world, special circumstances are necessary to encourage the meditative process. In our cities, filled with advertisements and traffic, the mass of color exacts a daily strain on one's visual capacities; an urgent need arises to rest one's eyes. The excessive demands by the ever-brutal dictatorship of color also result in a logical indifference to any "spartan celebration": so, environmental passivity turns out to be more than a stimulating starting point for a state in which the mind is active. Relating this to the non-colors, white and black—their positive character in opposition to the vehemence of red and yellow rests primarily in their weaker excitement potential.[6]

A lot of conjecture and writings have been brought forth about colors and their nature. But only a few have succeeded in their almost dissolute investigations in drawing a clear line between the factual and the purely hypothetical. Even Kandinsky is guilty here—in his definitions, the synesthetic metaphor plays a leading part. For example, in analyzing white, he tries repeatedly to capture the speechlessness of this non-color.[7] "That is why it has the effect on our psyche of a great silence, which for us is absolute. It has an inward sound of nothingness corresponding to many pauses in music." And he sees black as "nothing," with no potential, "like an eternal silence without future or hope." To him, black is "something extinguished, motionless, the stillness of the body after death." Rainer Volp, in a long-overdue publication, *Art as Symbol,* made crucial corrections on the distorted characters of colors and about the infantile association which the church maintained in its post-mortems on symbols, which were in great demand. Here for once, it is asserted that white, the first liturgically meaningful color, can, in today's art, no longer be kept simply as a symbol of worship. Volp also emphasizes its architectural and celebratory qualities, which I tried to characterize earlier in the word "exoneration." In the conclusion to his discourse on white—and this differentiates his work from many others—Volp states, in all modesty, that one can in fact only speak of white in an enduring symbolic sense—on a psychic *and* physical level where looking at a form creates realities which are relatively abstracted from institutionalized tradition, and that the ambivalence of color constantly calls for a reexamination of traditional values. Even the white or gray "window" lends itself to such scrutiny and evaluation.[8]

THE NEW CHANCE FOR A
SCALE OF LIGHT CHARACTER

But before I go on to talk about numerous important works in this field of art, we should take a quick look at the special characteristics of light membranes in an architectural context. Firstly, the peculiar consideration in the use of this form is the beneficial quality of lighting for a given room and the resulting illumination of architectural context.[9] Secondly, when the general proportion and subject matter of the building are not even affected by the distorting power of a strongly colored light, loss of reality is minimal. Finally, the glass walls in themselves suggest neither retreat nor approach; they stand firm and flat. This makes them building elements with which one can make precise calculations. In dialectic contrast with the regularity of the wall stands the white-gray skin of glass—like any other window, sabotaging first and foremost the notions of materialism and opaqueness associated with the actual phenomena of a wall.[10]

Naturally, the sparing use of color in *grisailles* creates a great degree of withdrawal and tranquility. Yet, it would be hasty to conclude that their lack of expressive color could leave one with an information vacuum which couldn't be suitably replaced. The modalities of illumination conjured up by various types of glass and the conscious gradations of transparency articulate colored light into specifically recognizable forms of expression, inachievable by any other method. It is, in fact, color that obstructs the perception of light transmission. The perspicacity of its demands overrides most of their presence.

So, light is dispersed through the "filter" of glass with its various effects. It either completely penetrates, comes up against the resistance of structural limitations, lingers on it, or is reflected back in the direction of its source. From there we see it in the form of shimmers, glints, glimmers, glows, beams, glitters, glares, and flashes.

Armed with this vocabulary of light characters applied to certain specialized types of glass in the form of a window, contemporary artists had opened up for themselves new possibilities, inaccessible to medieval glass artists. The use or rejection of that aesthetic quotation of light characters prejudges the basic form of most *grisailles* of this century.

REFLECTIONS OF POLARIZED TENSIONS OF CONTEMPORARY MAN

Only the systematic kindling of interest made it possible to progress from the slow pace of moderation of the unheard-of direct proclamation of glass and of the potential of uncovering its unique powers. By "uncover" I don't mean just the releasing of glass as a material from the necessary or even history-making intervention of a craftsman's work, but also its liberation from the literary and ideological bonds of the past.

After Josef Albers, in 1954, took the first step by making the altar window in the Abbey of St. John in Collegeville completely in white, Georg Meistermann caused a stir by designing the first all-white figurative window in Bad Kissingen in 1956.[11] The forms of two angels are fixed onto thick, opaque, white-glass panels in short, sharp flourishes resembling handwriting. The complete opaqueness means that there is a subdued light around the graphics, preventing any possible distraction from the design by outside factors. As soon after as 1958, Meistermann followed up with two abstract windows in the chancel of the chapel at Saarbrucken Castle. The most noticeable aspect of Meistermann's glass screens placed opposite each other is their streamlined and graphic character.[12] He avoids completely the play on tension which would result from using contrasting types of glass. The illumination of wall which, though perceptible, doesn't convey tangibility, is defined only by the absolute darkness of the lead. The contemplative mood of a room is actually an undynamic version of its appearance when subject to reduced light. One can experience the persuasiveness of such a stationary illumination in the old parish church of Ottweiler/Saar, which originated four years later. Their economical, black, perpendicular gestures correspond with the basic function of the organic breaks in geometrical repetition in my windows; this is particularly clear in the warm *grisailles* in the north aisle of St. Maria, Dortmund (1971–72).[13] In Ludwig Schaffrath's work, the imminent, static light from the opaque white combines fundamentally architectural objects so that the reflective walls for his windows in St. Michael's in Schweinfurt (1967–68)[14] and Tennenbronn (1968–70) are no longer a metaphor.[15]

It is self-explanatory that such a soft "plane" of light is especially conducive to objectively presenting frescoes or murals. This is proved by the successful outcome of Schaffrath's work for the Catholic Church in Bad Buchau by Federsee (1966), and Würzburg Cathedral (1965). Even then, the glass is slightly transparent, so its material density is emphasized, and the continuing illumination of the interior is guaranteed.[16] I am thinking here of Jochem Poensgen's windows in St. Jacob in Reuthe/Vorarlberg (1963), and Anton Wendling's small *grisailles* in the Doppelkirche Schwarz-Rheindorf (1957).[17] It is also this same introverted lighting effect which makes for the mildness of light in the main part of Boniface Church in Hofheim/Taunus (1968–69). The grayish-white shade of the wide west wall in this church is indeed amplified by an outside tone and, through this, borders on classical *grisaille* art. Strictly speaking, the westerly "glass frieze" in the monastery chapel at Leutesdorf cannot be counted as a pure white window, as its format is defined by two bands of blue.[18] Such definition of form was often practiced by medieval mural painters and book illustrators. I happen to share Kudielka's opinion that when current interests stimulate a glimpse into the past, a unique awareness of distance occurs without denying the present.[19] Such inquiries into the past aren't necessarily aimed at revival of traditions, but reflect a desire to retain freedom and choice in one's development in the face of the blind push towards everything new, while trying to metamorphose the past.

The exact opposite of the typically two-dimensional light[20] of opaque white or gray windows is seen in the unrestrained, three-dimensional glare of a plain window.[21] The use of what could be described as "open" glass is more favorable for a relatively unhindered passage of light. Plain windows live in unison with whatever is happening outside. The more transparent the glass, the more important are such background details, and the mobility is comprehended simultaneously with the art itself. And, most important: the opening of a closed-off space initiates its relativity; the act of letting in an unreduced light intensity transforms the structure of a room into a richly modulating "echo chamber." Anyone who wishes to experience such a fluctuating and fabulous light effect should see the cloisters of Aachen Cathedral, where Schaffrath supplemented the tracery corridors (1962–65) with free, veined lead work. I find that illustrations show the extent of the designer's involvement with, and consideration for, outside factors.[22] Otto Herbert Hajek goes so far as to allow daylight to penetrate the interior through plain glass in St. Mauritius, Weisbaden (1968). The view is split into geometrical segments by a powerful concrete division, and thus it is saved from its usual perception.[23] The conscious insertion of varying degrees of transparency also belongs to the category of true innovation. In a considerable number of great works, the alternating attraction and repulsion of real spatial references, the rejection and obliteration of misshapen remnants of reality develop into an autonomous "picture show" of great affinity.[24] The clash between the artistically perceived and the actual environment, or their careful, step-by-step merging becomes a theme in the material, and at the same time reflects, unconsciously, the polarized tensions from which contemporary man must pull through.

This drawing together of space and surface, of body and environment, is exemplified with remarkable clarity in Schaffrath's walls of light in the Church of St. Maria in Bad Zwischenahn (1970) and in the magnificent glass gables of Maria Rast in Aachen (1966).[25] There it reveals itself as a conflict between simple and tightly blown antique glass, a contrast of open glints and temperamental glares.[26]

In the windows of the Church of the Holy Cross in Soest by Buschulte (1968), or the Carmelite Monastery in Duren by Schaffrath (1964), the dynamic authenticity of bright light and glitter are exchanged for a more reserved partnership: the moving light of slightly opalized glasses is situated to contrast with the stationary light unique to opaque glass. In such windows, the differentiating factors are the characteristic changing of the opaque sections and the sudden transformations into contrary color tones, depending on background.[27]

THE ADVENTURE OF DIFFERING DEGREES
OF TRANSPARENCY IN COLORLESS GLASS

The fact that the differing degrees of light transparency in colorless panes accentuate relative degrees of brightness, and that a thoroughly white opaque glass, in the same context as white foam, can give the effect of gray when looked through against open sky, makes familiarity with varying types of glass an adventure.

If the outside environment in my vestry and other windows in the Catholic Church of Weiburn/Eifel (1968–69), or in the crypt windows of Maria Laach (1969), is there only as a shadowy "warning",[28] in Schaffrath's prismatic windows, the outside environment's escape into the realms of light defies description. Here, aided and abetted by the sparkling of crystalline glass, the outside environment is playing tricks; fragments of reality are wantonly parodied and distorted at the slightest movement of the observer. In the broken-edged effect of concrete and glass windows which still retain their profusion of sporadic unfathomable flame, the fire of rows of prisms makes for a complex arrangement of artificially controlled light.[29] While Schaffrath puts his "oases" of light among opaque white "masonry," he stresses their kinetic relationship. From time to time in his white windows, the active fulguration is only realized as tiny, penetrating, clear lenses[30] which then crop up in homeopathic doses and technoid groupings, as demonstrated in the Chapel of St. John in Essen Cathedral (1968).[31] The fact that three-dimensional prisms can be included in a monolithic opaque sheet of plexiglass and thereby seem to hover freely within the square is shown by my *grisailles* in the Ebert collection in Kleinwallstadt (1973). The spontaneous pattern of the lead, a primary facet of my windows, stands here in energetic opposition to the regularities of the architecture and, at the same time, records the salient strength of the light and its destructive possibilities.

BANALITIES ON A NEW PLAN MADE INTO POETRY

Finally, one of the most talked about ingredients in contemporary *grisailles* is the mechanically produced ornamental glass. Dominikus Bohm was the first to use it in a sacred environment as early as 1953, in the mighty south wall of Marcia the Queen in Köln-Marienburg.[32] Far be it from me to belittle this work in any way; nevertheless, I am in agreement with Herbert Muck, S.J., who traces the outgoing "magic" of this wall to the fact that it awakes in many respects a similar 'cosmic' feeling as ancient mosaics and early Christian jewelled tapestries, and maintains that this effect is attributable to the sparkling stereotyped surface stamping of the glass.

However, Dominikus Bohm broke through an aesthetic and ideological wall by this means; and as early as 1956, H.A.P. Grieshaber followed with a rustic frieze in the Catholic Church at Metzingen, a pleasant exception to the countless figurative anachronisms unfortunately demanded everywhere by churches after the war.[33] The last work known to me in the series of pure industrial glass was designed by Hans Ostendorf in St. Barbara's at Gelsenkirchen, Rotthausen (1969). This consists of revolving rows of perpendicular glass laminae which pick up and transmit light and shade in rich formations.[34]

Thus Bohm, Grieshaber, and Ostendorf did a necessary thing. They refused to conform to the defeatist prejudices of aesthetic grumblers who are interested only in the incompatability of art with mass production. Instead, they coaxed their own artistic modalities out from the banalities of machine-made aesthetics onto a new plane and made them into a piece of poetry. I am firmly convinced that such artistic relationships are our best chance to reconcile the divergence of machine and men and finally to soothe the neurotic relationship between man and mass production.

Let us close our discourse with three unique examples which have been completely ignored in this writing. The close proximity of modern inclinations in art and its high degree of material rejection make them just as much "timeless" as "of our time." Instead of imposing a preconceived idea on the material, Gangkofner, Ostendorf, and Holweck develop their concept in direct contact with the medium, therefore, the success of the final work depends on the essential mastering of the material, rather than being a rough approximation of an idea.

The remarkable thing about all three designers is their unanimous trust in the true qualities of light. Alios Gangkofner delivers himself entirely to this trust when raising the element to an artistic plane in his faultless columns of prisms, illustrated in his glass-relief memorial to those killed in the war in Munich.[35] He goes further than the obvious brilliancy to achieve an appearance of transoptical value despite the strict geometry and ruthless precision of the colorless crystal glass polished on both sides, which disperses the sunlight into the spectral colors and allows them to wander like a polymorphous ornament in a prescribed movement across the concrete sections of the wall.

Similarly, the richly varied orthogonal glass reliefs by Hans Ostendorf in the Church of the Holy Cross at Glasbeck-Butendorf (1965–66) defy adequate description. Only the eye can appreciate the light potential in this plain glass.[36]

Finally, there is the unforgettable mixture of light in the huge Maria-Hilf Church in Fechingen/Saar, the walls of which are by Oskar Holweck (1962–64).[37] They consist of segments fixed one above the other sloping 45 degrees downwards; a rhythmical change is achieved by making every fourth gap a "light sluice." The distance which the indirect light has to cover begins at the blue ceramic surfaces of the segments. From here it is reflected onto the white base of the respective segments above, and is finally reflected into the room as a soft blue. The alternating crescendo and diminishing of this deeply metaphysical light and the staggering simplicity of Holweck's artistic method unite here to form a feeling of maximum tranquility.

As we are at the end of this exposition, I will allow myself to pronounce the contribution of contemporary *grisaille* to be a process of leading man back to his origins, a striking indication of the exhausting emptiness necessary before we can return to an awareness of undiminished realities.[38]

GOOD BEHAVIOR AND BAD TASTE

PATRICK REYNTIENS

The history of any official art inevitably becomes the history of failure or success in methods of control—control by the client. True, this may ultimately be reduced to a question of taste, but taste essentially as revealing the nature of the client, rather than that of the art.[1] The distinction and struggle between that art which is commissioned and that which is freely conceived by the artist has been around a long time, as we know from the letters of Giovanni Bellini to Poliziano; but, there is no doubt that it has become far more marked, involving far more polarity, during the last hundred years. In these days, when the role of the artist has shifted ground from a duty, hitherto largely unquestioned, to give expression to society, toward ground that looks suspiciously similar to that of the artist *as alchemist*, it is practically impossible to combine these two divergent positions, still less to blunt the distinction between them. The artist, in Paul Klee's dictum, does assume the role of alchemist, and the painter or sculptor becomes the prophet or seer—dealing in values that are as life-enhancing in proportion as they are inexplicable.[2] In such a situation, any kind of direct control of the artist by the client is unpopular and is not to be admitted, and it eventually becomes an impossibility. Acquiescence to such control, if it existed, is inconceivable: after all, artistic freedom of experiment, like the scientific freedom of experiment that it echoes, is unattached to any particular goal set by any agency outside the artist. This situation may be universal in all arts save those of journalism and film-music— and perhaps architecture—but it is undoubtedly the most appropriate and convenient one for the artist vis-a-vis the plural society—a society without sharp focus and definite goals (apart from the utile), and whose appetites largely tend to deny its aspirations—a society seemingly waiting for a God out of its own Machine.

It is this world situation that the main commissioning bodies of stained glass, the Churches, have to contend with. From some points of view they are anachronistic to a degree; from others they seem to offer the hope of an existence of more friendship, fraternity, and integrity than we all possess at the moment—and perhaps the future will indeed force us to reconsider the implicit social and psychological values that the Churches offer.

Now, it is one thing to make generalizations; it is another to fit these into the particular scene with its existential situation and make sense of it all. A review of the relative position of the Churches in England, after some further explanation of this situation in France and Germany, is essential if we are to make sense at all of past achievements and aims and assess these against future possibilities.

In a penetrating sermon on Laud, the greatest of the Anglican Archbishops of Canterbury in the seventeenth century, Professor R.W. Southern makes a salient point and, in doing so, comes close to defining the ethos of the Church of England. Laud's policy was, "firstly, to restore and preserve order and stability in society in the face of a rising tide of dissent and disorder, and secondly, to bring English thought and learning back into the mainstream of its European tradition after a century of confusion and insularity." True, Laud was only given some twenty years to do this, as the sermon makes plain, and the task was manifestly impossible for one man to accomplish in a lifetime; but, by the time he died something momentous had been achieved. The Church of England had received an image, an ineradicable stamp, from his efforts, and henceforth would be known both by her members and by her friends without, as well as by her enemies, as a society primarily concerned with the maintenance of good order and quietness; a quietness that encompasses good behavior. This has little enough to do with doctrine and practically nothing to do with ecclesiastical authority. It is largely a question of ethos. On that plane, the Church of England represents English society on its *best behavior,* and is a reflection of that central fixity of the English temperament in its determination not to rock the boat. It has already been said that this ethos has nothing to do with doctrine or dogma, but the Church of England is not an ideological society either, because the Engish themselves are not a people motivated by ideas. The reason for this is that England has never suffered the experience of deprivation and deep dislocation. Only those who have suffered some kind of deep-rooted alienation are susceptible to ideology, and English society, broadly speaking, has not suffered in this severe psychological and social way since the middle of the sixteenth century.

This, in part, does something to explain why the splendors and miseries of modern art alike are so rare in the area covered by Church patronage; they are ideological. In some way, the idea of modern art is still vaguely suspect and continental—possibly Russian and revolutionary—and still, to the uninitiated, it connotes acute-angled drawing and fiercely abutting colors. This image of innovative art is admittedly some fifty years out of date, but surprisingly it still exists and is very prevalent. What is not surprising is that, in their turn, modern artists of whatever complexion, should find a society on its best behavior both incomprehensible and uncongenial. Such a society has no appeal. The examples of modern art in the Church of England are very few.

Apart from Coventry Cathedral, now well encapsulated in history, and one or two enterprising parish churches, most of the stained glass that has been commissioned in the last twenty years and that falls outside the genre of "safe"—what John Betjeman has termed "making a fortune out of the tasteless and bereaved"[3]—has been commissioned by private foundations or for private individuals. The Church of England as an official commissioning body has always found it more convenient and appropriate to commission from men of impeccable craftsmanship, but timid, if not deficient, artistic vision. This emphasis may well arise as a result of the predominant background of the Church, one which has always used *decorum* to cover its lack of clear thinking regarding the relative positions and merits of "principle" and "quantum:" a deficiency of *fond* leads to an emphasis on *forme.* The idea of Laud's "good order" persists as ever, and the ideal is still one of stasis, clarity, and calm. The results are frequently so bland and innocuous as to attract no one; but they are guaranteed to offend no one either.

In contrast to the Church of England, the Roman Catholic Church in England is, and always has been, a highly ideological society. Even after a hundred and fifty years of emancipation, it is plain that the "Italian Mission" has not lost its internal conviction of being in the right. The commissioned glass, as other art, in Catholic churches reflects, more often than not, the conviction and taste of the clergy, rather than that of the laity; the opposite being true of the Church of England. It is worth considering whether, in these ecumenical days, the exceedingly pointed things said of the other Church by such expert apologists as Dean Inge on the one side, and Cardinal Newman on the other, should not be reexamined with a view to applying them in the sphere of taste and ethos, however softened their impact may have become in the spheres of theology and authority by this time. Certainly, after a hundred and fifty years of emancipation, the Catholic Church in England has neither succeeded in feeling the tempo of England, nor in feeling the "feeling" of England. Thankfully, one factor intervenes which, because of its slowness, may do a lot of good. The Catholic Church, in spite of popular conviction to the contrary, is, comparatively speaking, very poor. This is a blessing since there is no knowing what her basic lack of taste might innocently inflict on the British public were she rich. Lacking in feeling and touch and taste as she may be, the Catholic Church is not attached to any particular *ethos:* she is not on her "best behavior." The Catholic Church is unequivocal: her fundamental ideology is never in doubt; and though this may mean that dogmatic barriers ward off much potential contact with the achievements of modern art, when the two do come together successfully, the result can be of great satisfaction and significance. But, this most rarely happens in England—far more often abroad.

It is not certain that the Nonconformist Churches in England understand visual art at all, except as an expression of some sort of moral probity. Hence, the plainer the building, the better the art—the more satisfactory to the human spirit. Shaker art is the ultimate ideal of the nonconformist conscience and this is deeply moving. But the idea and use of cultural and religious metaphor is not understood, and there is an historical explanation for this. The artistic ideas of nonconformists spring from the maturation of the Puritan conscience in the sixteenth century, and from the revulsion from conspicuous display as typified by Jacobean and Caroline upper-class society in the early seventeenth century. The Laudian and Arminian Churches, which inevitably were the outward expression of such an upper-class society, became victims of this movement of revulsion. After all, there was no attraction for Puritans in an elaborate structure of symbolism and metaphor that seemed overblown, insincere, part pagan, and certainly grossly extravagant.[4] In any case, the fundamental egalitarianism of nonconformists would make it extremely difficult to embody *any* art of metaphor or symbolism in any form, even if the roles were understood. Nonconformist patronage of the visual arts from every point of view seems to be a non-starter: the mental prerequisites for participation simply are not in evidence.

What all the main groups of Christian thinking hold in common is, however, a quality of awareness, perception, and thought which is quite alien to modern society. Although the Churches differ in emphasis and depth, their modes of thought are based on deeply held memory systems and on far-flung eschatologies. Both these phenomena are intensely alien to modern society and its ways of thinking. In the latter context, a Christian eschatology in a post-Christian world becomes an intrinsic absurdity, even when held at its most tentative. For secular society, taken as a whole, there remains only a kind of *personal* eschatology which is of little importance or significance to persons outside the immediate circle of friends and relations. Any *social* eschatology that might persist is usually thought of in terms of some kind of anticipated reordering of society, perhaps a vaguely chiliastic urge; but, this is more often channeled down materialist tracks laid by Michelet, Compte, Darwin, Spencer, Marx, and other popular materialist philosophers in the nineteenth century.

Memory, in a world that has devised means of communication and storing of data giving immediate and well-nigh infinite total recall, has perhaps inevitably had its role in society drastically revised. In her remarkable book, *The Art of Memory,* Frances Yates quotes St. Thomas Aquinas as holding, apparently uniquely, that the act of memory is a moral *act.*[5] The memorative act is not merely a mechanical act, as modern technology and applied science would have it be, but has an extra dimension. This dimension penetrates to the interior identity of the psyche where it finds its probity and reason for being; en route it ensures the common foundation of shared experience from which it is possible to construct a concept with true meaning outside the individual conceiving it. The act of memory being *moral* implies that the selective screening process of what is and what is not remembered has an intimate and vital relationship with the psyche engaged in the memorative act. The question of anamnesis immediately arises when this idea of memory and its connection to mental concepts is applied to art. True, to a greater or lesser extent all art is anamnesic, but anamnesis in Christian art could be described as an indwelling moral quality without which the artifact could not exist. Now, nothing could be more alien to the spirit of twentieth-century art in general than what has just been described.

Twentieth-century art has indeed a memorative content, but this, more often than not, is strictly in relation to the artist as a being in himself; or perhaps as a representative of all single human beings (as he is presented on mass media, through television and cheap reproductions); or again, as a representative of the spectator's other ego—

more usually the inarticulate and subconscious ego, now brought forth and shown publicly in an act of self-revelation. The public waits for a revelation from the artist. Again, twentieth-century art is not related to specific time and place, and still less to society, and in these circumstances the act of anamnesis is bound to become a personal revelation. Because it is so personal, it is dangerously implacable in its demands, and, *because* of its hermetic basis, all but incontrovertible. In these circumstances, the personal revelation overflows into a kind of antinomianism[6] and the revolution in communications makes it possible for the most hermetic and antinomian systems to gain credence, if only for a time, as supposedly universally comprehensible systems of values; but, more often than not, disillusion sets in after a lapse of time. Nowadays, thanks to communication techniques, antinomianism can assume the character of a *non-church,* really effectively for the first time. Nevertheless, the vast majority of viewers of television still seem to distrust the content and the form of such modern art, and it may be that the very absence of an in-depth memorative content is fundamentally alien to the thought patterns and habits that human beings have acquired over thousands of years.

The polarity between the highly personal and intensified work of sculpture and painting and the bland and impersonal *matière* and expression of modern architecture is only too obvious. The whole museum system stretching over the world imposes its assumptions and standards on society so that the work of art automatically seems, in the act of being placed in a museum, to assume the nature of an instant ethnographic exhibit.[7] However, the principle of Peripatesis immediately comes into play, and so long as the work of art is kept constantly on the move and the display changing, the idea of a correspondence with a supposedly healthy consumer society is upheld. Peripatesis leads directly to kinesis, and the kinetic assumes the role of the memorative: what should be anchored into the center of the psyche is destroyed in favor of a serial image that takes the place of memory. Perhaps the ultimate example of this is that of television— the flickering image, preposterously colored, in its smooth impersonal packaging. The serious position of an artist whose role it is to produce works of art with a highly anamnesic quality, in contiguity to—in actual physical communication with—a work of architecture, which has no concern at all with the anamnesic, will now be fully appreciated. The anomaly is inescapable.

Leading on from what has been indicated concerning the memorative, it can easily be demonstrated that the Churches are the only major units within the plural society that are still concerned in depth with what could be called "organic memory." That is, they are concerned with the structure of memory having a nature such that, if any part of it is set aside or ignored, it could lead to the collapse of the consciousness, and therefore, of the whole life of the Church as an identifiable society. Other constituent parts of the plural society are not so vulnerable, since they merely treat the memorative process as a convenience, incidentally more and more relegated to machines.[8]

Owing to general noncomprehension of this problem (it is, after all, a very deep cleavage between modes of apprehension), the Churches have, largely falsely, been charged with excessive conservatism. But this is to see the whole question in far too shallow a way; it is not necessarily a matter of innate conservatism so much as an appreciation of the necessity of making the memorative act a moral act (as St. Thomas pointed out), rather than a superficial mechanical convenience. This inevitably leads to slowness and caution which can be misinterpreted as conservatism. The misapprehension of this fact leads the Catholic Church, for instance, to be accused of siding with the dictatorships of the Right (at various times in the twentieth century in Austria, Germany, Italy, Spain, Portugal, and South America), who *themselves* are seeking to use the organic memory process, or a caricature of it, illicitly—for purposes of gaining political power.

This political situation is a comparatively recent phenomenon, probably traceable to the general upheaval following the French Revolution and the Napoleonic era.[9] The latter twenty years of the eighteenth century and the first twenty years of the nineteenth century coincided with the Industrial Revolution, and this was followed rapidly by the *educational* revolution and, in time, the *communication* revolution, in Western Europe and North America. During this period of the nineteenth century, these successive revolutions modified the world outlook and supplied the ferment, the dynamism, out of which most of the possibilities in modern painting and sculpture arose. Coincidental to these social and political movements and contributory to them, was the final emancipation of European Jewry from the mental and physical confinement in ghettos. This emancipation gave the first opportunity for Jews to approach a serious point of leverage vis-à-vis contemporary Western society. Owing to hundreds of years of repression, this leverage was used sometimes to redress grievances and injustices that occurred particularly in Russia and Eastern Europe (many political revolutionaries were understandably Jewish) and to gain considerable control over the economic, scientific, political, and financial destinies of countries such as France, Germany, and America. This, from the point of view of the present essay, was an interesting phenomenon which perhaps has not been noticed before: for the first time in over a thousand years, since the Christianization of the Roman Empire, Western society was influenced and modified by a factor both material and psychological that, by force of circumstances, was still constrained to preserve its memory structure (the Jewish faith) strictly and hermetically sealed against an exterior society, while at the same time set free to experiment for the first time in dextrous, and sometimes ruthless, pragmatism within that society.[10] The ultimate reason for this anomalous situation lay partly, perhaps, in the hypocrisy of the various Churches through their being too closely attached to the then sources of political power, and in their pretending that nineteenth-century society in general was still Christian, resulting in the manipulation of the popular religious prejudices by secular regimes for the purposes of their own power. One only need instance the Russian pogroms of the late nineteenth century or the individual case of Dreyfus in France to see this principle at work. Christians were guilty of having no compassion for the Jews as *human beings,* and almost worse, no spirit of inquiry towards the achievements of latter-day Jewish teaching which might have led them to understand the situation more deeply. When Christian compassion came (1940–44), it was too late.

By people outside the European and English traditions it is not always realized how widely different are the histories of the individual Churches in Western European countries. The situation and the historical background of the Church in France differs markedly from that in Germany, and therefore has a profound influence on the kind of patronage possible there and on the art resultant from that patronage.

In France in the early twentieth century, after its complete and ruthless dispossession by the State, the Roman Catholic Church was in a position at once of great weakness and great strength. By secularization, the idea of Christianity had been severed from the State; this absolved the Church of any feelings of complicity with sins of commission or omission on the State's part.

But, emancipated as it was, the Church was divided between, on the one hand, the "organic" *vieille France* of *tradition* (of Charles Maurras) and, on the other, the exceedingly brilliant spiritual and intellectual revival of Péguy, Leon Bloy, Maritain, Gabriel Marcel, and Paul Claudel. These last made full use of the freedom and emancipated position of the Church to pursue inquiries with all that could be fruitful for the Church in the modern movement in art, literature, and philosophy. To a large extent, this movement was dominated in France, as in the rest of Europe, by brilliant and emancipated Jewish intellectuals. Again, the greater part of the intellectual and artistic movements of *La Belle Epoque* and after, with the possible exception of music, was dominated in Paris by expatriates, many of whom were of Eastern European Jewish origin. It is from these encounters that the courage and perspicacity of the Church in France springs in having commissioned the works of art and architecture which have contributed to its renown as a real instrument of the best of twentieth-century civilization. It remains to be seen if the deprivation of material resources at the beginning of this century will have the lasting effect of denying full expression, in a material way, to the intellectual and spiritual vision of the Church's emancipated life in France.

In contrast to France, the Roman Catholic Church in West Germany has been, for the last three decades, in a unique and, by force of circumstances, considerably privileged, position. When Germany was defeated by the Western Allies in 1945, a factor of enormous significance came into play: the political decision to split Germany into two parts. For the first time in one hundred and fifty years, the Catholic Rhineland, the upper Rhine, and Bavaria were able to break away from the political and cultural dominance of Prussia and Berlin and demonstrate a political ethos and ideal which was far more akin to the Goethean ethos of eighteenth-century Germany, i.e., an ethos untainted by authoritarian militarism. Modern Western Germany could not have arisen without the willing consent of the Catholic Church. Indeed, at the total collapse of Nazism in 1945, the Allies did all in their power to fill up the dangerous cultural gap in the political scene by encouraging anything to take over, provided it was not Communism. The Catholic Church benefited principally because , weak as she was, she seems to have been the only major quasi-political factor in society still left standing at the time, and the Christian Democratic Party consequently was ahead of any other political party in its organization and plans. The result is the high degree of Church or confessional allegiance in present-day Germany and the success, from a fiscal, if not a spiritual point of view, of the Church tax system.

The expansion of such a church movement, which is at once social and political, is now largely manifest in the architecture and the decoration of confessional buildings, such as Catholic and Lutheran Churches, schools, convents, hospitals, old peoples' homes, and social centers. All these buildings tend to extend the initial opportunities offered to the stained-glass artist in Germany—and these are opportunities unparallelled in the rest of the world.

When the Second World War ended, the German Church, Catholic and Lutheran, seemed to have found itself in a curious position. Catastrophic urban devastation almost forced the Church to make use of the new art forms that had nothing to do with the remote or immediate past in order to reiterate the timeless message of salvation. In architecture, much had to be built very quickly, and there was plenty of opportunity for experiment. The anomalous result seems to have been that an *am*nesic art (that is, *non*associational, *non*representational, *non*historical), had the purpose of recommending and expressing the beliefs of a society whose very nature was bound up with the opposite, i.e., *an*amnesis. A lesser irony lay in the impossibility of employing any art forms with allusions either to Nazi Germany or Weimar or Imperial aesthetics or ethics (even had Germans wanted to use them which, understandably, they did not). Germany, to this day, is the victim of an enforced amnesia—enjoined equally by her own conscious break with her immediate past, and by her realizing that this "forgetfulness" is a *sine qua non,* imposed on her by her conquerors-turned-partners in the European experiment. Such a state of suspended inquiry cannot be for the mental good of *any* nation, let alone Germany.

As a result of the uncertain interiority of the individual, the art forms flourishing in Germany are not exactly those expressing individual emancipation, but rather those which express social adhesion; that is, public art forms. A look at history will surely prove that this inclination to the social has always, in fact, been evident in Germany. Looking backward from the period of the Nazi era, through the Rococo and the Baroque to the High Gothic and the Romanesque, all periods have been concerned with art forms primarily as an expression of *public* self-confidence and identity, however gifted the actual individual practicing them might have been. It could be said with justice that the genius of German art lies in just this fact. Germany has a genius for art on a social scale, though much of it does not rise above a certain standard. Consequently, in Germany, society does support art in a way and on a scale that is unparalleled and unthinkable in England or even North America, and moreover, backs its moral support by legislation regarding taxation and tax deduction that makes such support effective. The question remains: does society control the art resulting? The answer is yes. What the Church *is* concerned with coincides with the aims of society, and that is to encourage the successful application of the achievements of modern art (primarily nonfigurative painting) to a general situation, vis-à-vis society. As a consequence, the result may be of relatively low aesthetic pressure, but it happens to be efficiently spread throughout society in general. Individual conviction behind much modern German stained glass seems in many cases lacking, but the level of the art is sustained by the force of the movement as a whole.

This is by no means to deny the real achievement of the German post-war accomplishments: it remains the most powerful movement in European decorative art; but, it is still a social movement in art rather than a collection of individual achievements. In contrast to this general "social" achievement of Germany, the achievement of the Church in France should be seen rather as a liberal commissioning of what are, to all intents and purposes, "private" works of art. The individual French achievements are abounding in vitality in themselves, but they are isolated both from each other and from society. They remain a collection of individual works.

It has been demonstrated that in England the problem of commissioning stained glass is inextricably bound up with the ethos of a class structure holding powers of patronage. Churches have become not so much illustrations of the vanguard of modern achievement as the expression of the mood of a certain section of society.

But, there is another and more fundamental difference in the political situation. Whereas in Europe the Church has taken, for the better or worse, a far more defined political stance, this has always been avoided in England, with the result that the Church is in a position of isolation concerning cultural matters. It could be summed up simply as: no political definition, no effective leverage on culture. The contrast of England to Spain, Germany, Holland, and Belgium in this matter is extreme. This political fact poses interesting questions for the future. Should the Church opt to go into a political scene with all the attendant risks and opportunities, or to withdraw from the central scene with the risk of becoming irrelevant to the life of the country and beginning to exhibit the symptoms of the art of an ethnic minority? This is an interesting dilemma, but one that may be relieved of its acuteness by the growing tendency in society to question the very basis and tenets of the modern movement. Perhaps in this new, fluid situation there will be cause for some hope.

AUTONOMY AS A
SPURIOUS ABSOLUTE

ROBERT SOWERS

The contemporary stained-glass artist, spurned for his inability to deal with traditional subjects in the traditional manner, may find himself taken to task, sometimes by the same critics, for an opposite failing. Because his work is normally commissioned, must relate to a given space, and may even be called upon to evoke, however implicitly, some particular range of human experience—because it is an "applied" art—it is declared to be hopelessly compromised from the outset. In effect, the autonomy of art, its utter freedom from any possible link with any place, thing, or function outside itself is raised to the level of a quasi-moral absolute: "The one assault on fine art is the ceaseless attempt to subserve it as a means to some other end or value. The one fight in art is not between art and non-art, but between true and false art, between pure art and action-assemblage art, between abstract and surrealist—expressionist anti-art, between free art and servile art. Abstract art has its own integrity, not someone else's 'integration' with something else. Any combining, mixing, adding, diluting, exploiting, vulgarizing, or popularizing abstract art deprives art of its essence and depraves the artist's conscience. Art is free, but it is not a free-for-all . . . Artists who claim their work comes from nature, life, reality, earth, or heaven, as 'mirrors of the soul' or 'reflections of conditions' or 'instruments of the universe,' who cook up 'new-images-of-man' figures and 'nature-in-abstraction' pictures, are, subjectively and objectively, rascals and rustics."[1] Thus wrote Ad Reinhardt, the late New York school painter who rose to prominence in the 1960s as the militant conscience of minimal art. Even after due allowance is made for his satirical intent, the attitudes expressed in this statement remain a potent force in the art world, a dense thicket of assumption whereby the whole enterprise of the stained-glass artist stands massively condemned. It is, therefore, time to examine these assumptions, point by point, with full Reinhardtian rigor.

AUTONOMY AS A SPURIOUS ABSOLUTE

What about the artist who accepts a commission, to start with one of his chief bugbears? How can the artist possibly promise to deliver art to order? Far from being in any sense culturally constructive, is this not simply false yea-saying, the artist witlessly making common cause with the whole syndrome of boosters, bible-bangers, white-collar inspirationists and culture consultants, and the public to whom they peddle their various gratifications for low fun and high profits?

The answer is that it is not always, nor is it by any means necessarily or exclusively, that and that alone. Is every patron so simple-minded and every artist who accepts a commission so venal that the understanding between them must be the artist's absolute guarantee to deliver just the sought-for culture goods, on the barrelhead? Given the least bit more charitable interpretation, may it not be understood that a commission—or even the sponsorship of an artist by a gallery, for that matter—is rather a shared risk? Is it not, at least sometimes, a perfectly genuine effort to facilitate the creation of art by combining the talents of one man with the material resources of another? That appears to be how Daniel-Henrey Kahnweiler and the young Picasso, Sergei Shchukin, and Matisse understood it, at any rate.

Or take away every vestige of the patron's good intentions, however well- or ill-founded. Suppose he is some coarse and capricious bully boy on the cultural make, someone with no clue about art, bent on pure self-aggrandizement. Even in such extreme situations, the die is not always cast against the artist and his art. The crucial point—as Alberti, as Michelangelo, as Mozart, and countless other artists have always known—is whether, given the proffered resources, the artist can see any possibility for the legitimate exercise of his abilities; and whether he can or cannot just be as much a measure of his own stature as anything else.

Or even this may be conceded and a case still made: is there not something opportunistic, something finally shoddy about catering, however indirectly, to such motivations regardless of one's own private intentions? If there is, some surprising heads must roll; but justice, after all, is blind. Should not Abbot Suger's architect, observing the vulgar streak, the weakness for sheer opulence in his patron, have refused to work for him? Should not his successors in Chartres, Bourges, and Amiens, to say nothing of Beauvais, have refused to associate themselves with what was so obviously, among other things, a matter of out-and-out municipal rivalry? Should not Michelangelo have stuck to his guns and refused altogether to paint the Sistine ceiling? Are we not disgusted with Shakespeare and Beethoven because of the gross plebeians for whom they performed their works? Or Goya because he consented to paint portraits of a bunch of royal imbeciles? Or with Matisse, Léger, and Le Corbusier for working for the Church? Quite possibly the only thing that such greats have in common with much, much lesser men is that they seldom trouble themselves about such matters unduly.

In fact, just how scrupulous *can* the artist be about the motives of those who may be in a position to "use" his art? But, grant for the sake of the argument that this really is a matter of vital concern—that the artist must never, under any circumstances, allow anyone to wring an ounce of false gratification from his work. Commissions are then absolutely out of the question on the grounds that, no matter how capable the artist may be, or free to do what he likes, or how excellent his achievement, some use of his work is all but inherent in the fact of its being commissioned—some degree of do-gooding on the part of the patron or servility on his own part, if not both. Whoever chooses to be this rigorous about the matter has every right to do so; but then we may fairly expect him to be no less concerned about the dangers that lurk elsewhere.

Since no one can tell what lurid composts of cultural self-improvement, chic apocalypse-chasing, and naked speculation exists in the mind of the average collector, putting one's works in the hands of a dealer is surely out of the question. Any money gotten from sales to jet-set sharpies, corporate Medicis, or flint-eyed art speculators would be dirty money, filthy lucre. The artist must therefore forsake all commerce with galleries and wait, if not for posterity, for the museums to seek out his work. Yet doubts must still plague the minds of the totally scrupulous, since museums, after all, are run by curators who, on the evidence of the past, have not only refused the donation of masterpieces, but spent inordinate sums of money on pure junk. The artist, then, who accepts even museums must do so reluctantly—presumably on the grounds that they are the least sullied refuge for art in a grossly imperfect world. But he has utterly capitulated on the matter of the patron's motives.

All real art then belongs, somewhat grudgingly, in this least tarnished place and nowhere else. What kind of world does this injunction bring to mind, this world in which the one place for art as art, the one place where one might cleanse one's soul, is the museum of fine art? What shall exist outside this mausoleum of utter "soundlessness, timelessness, airlessness and lifelessness'' except a world of total ugliness, from roadtown disembowelments to decorator's and institutional pomp and circumstance, since no artist worthy of the name shall ever dare to lift a finger in it for fear of besmirching the good name of art?

If there is any legitimate relation between any work of art and any public, it is not a relation that develops quite independently of the location or ownership of those works, nor of whether the work in question is a whole autonomous work—like the *Colleoni* in Venice; or part of a larger work, like some figure on the Royal Portal of Chartres; or the mere fragmentary remains of some work, like a Greek torso. Do not such works always speak to some people with a wondrous delight whether they are seen in a public square or a private collection, in a museum or the jungles of Cambodia?

So much then, for the proscription that art *must not* be used. We come now to the far more radical assertion that art *cannot* be used: "The one meaning in art as art, past or present, is art meaning. When an art object is separated from its original time and place and use and is moved into the art museum, it gets emptied and purified of all its meanings except one. A religious object that becomes a work of art in an art museum loses all its religious meanings. No one in his right mind goes to an art museum to worship anything but art, or to learn about anything else."[2]

Simply tautological, if not false on all counts, the meanings of art are seldom if ever purely and simply meanings of art as art. How can we be sure that they ever are? But, assuming that they sometimes are, they are not the same meanings when the art object is separated from its original time and place and use and moved from *anywhere* to anywhere else. A painting that is framed no longer means the same thing that it meant on the easel; nor the same thing hanging on the wall as it means leaning against a wall; nor the same thing in a one-man show that it means in a group show nor may later mean in a retrospective; nor the same thing on one wall rather than another wall in any given show; nor the same as any of these things on the walls of a collector's living room, dining room, bedroom, cocktail bar, yacht, picture gallery or private chapel, or the walls of any public place. An art object that becomes an object of cult in a house of worship may well, for the worshipper, lose all of its meanings except one. On the other hand, no art lover in his right mind goes into any commercial gallery, private mansion, cathedral, Rathaus, emperor's boudoir, Queen's collection, painter's studio, or anywhere else to worship anything but art, or to learn about anything else, if it is art that he is out to worship.

While the work of art does not mean the same thing in any particular place or mind as in any other, it nevertheless has but one particular range or spectrum of possible meanings, different from that of any other creation, to the degree that it is intrinsically different or unique as an entity in its own right. To say that the work of art cannot be used is less accurate than to say that it is nearly always used in some way or other, and that while some uses of it may well be perverse, ignoble, or depraved, others are normal, necessary, or even on occasion inspired. In the one-thousand-year-old effort of the medieval church to employ art purely in the service of religion, one finds nothing half so relentlessly systematized, nothing so forced and stultifying as the academic ideal of "correctness," whose imperious tone finds its echo in Reinhardt's parlor strictures—and that ideal was born in an age of Fine Art.

ART OR ANTI-ART

JOHN PIPER

Twenty five years ago, in the early '50s, the painter Alfred Manessier was quoted as saying that he had come to believe less and less in stained-glass window designing, more and more in the simultaneous creation of a light-filled architectural unit, thought-out and created by a painter at one go. This statement echoed a conviction of my own, and I took to it at once and have always acted on it in considering how to go about any stained-glass project. The painter who has to do the thinking out and creating "at one go" may himself be the subsequent craftsman-maker, or the maker may be an inspired craftsman-interpreter who sees the point and interprets the "one-go" idea as a creative translator. Patrick Reyntiens and I have worked together on windows since 1950. He is himself a painter, and I have been specially lucky in this association because of his sensitive and inventive craftsmanship and his total understanding of the painterly approach. We are also lucky to have been at work in a period when more church building was going on than at any other time since the Middle Ages.

One has become conscious, during this period, of a collective consciousness that has grown up about the function of stained glass in relation to architecture—a contemporary consciousness, but one that also bears on stained glass of the past. This function is, above all, to qualify or alter the light, and hence to create a different atmosphere in a building or a room, and not necessarily to provide a message or even bright color. The messages of the windows at Chartres—their meaning as a Bible for the illiterate—has little significance for us in comparison with their transforming effect on the architecture of the interior, their creation of an enclosed, escapist world of color and modified light. We leave it to the scholars to interpret the messages and point out the morals, as we leave it to them to clean the glass and so arrest its decay, and incidentally to make the messages clearer, nearer to what they were originally, but not more beautiful. It seems likely that the early artists, being artists, would have delighted in their present state (before cleaning) and would be as pleased as we are with the effects of age and weathering. Robert Sowers in one of his books quotes Bernard Berenson as wondering "how much art, as distinct from mere craft, there is in our best twelfth- and thirteenth-century stained-glass windows. Their pattern is not easy to decipher, so much is it melted into the color: and when deciphered, how inferior it is in appeal!"[1] I have seen windows, not mere fragments, but entire windows, from St. Denis removed from the interior they were intended to transfigure, and I confess that one's enjoyment of them thus isolated was not so different from the Rajah's gloating over handfuls of emeralds, rubies, and other precious stones.

When, some years ago, we were asked to provide a memorial window for a London Church that has ranges of fine traceried windows in each of its spacious aisles, I asked, "which window?" I was told, "any one of them; whichever you think best." Except for a splendid east window, there is no stained glass in the church, old or modern. After a lot of thought and conversation with the sympathetic and enlightened incumbent, it was decided to appeal for somewhat larger funds and provide glass for all the windows on the south side: glass that was not at all aggressive or even particularly personal, but that would quietly modify the light in the body of the church—glass of careful design (greatly enhanced by Reyntiens' virtuoso leading), varying each window—and in gentle yellows, greens, whites, and silver grays. I think few visitors notice these windows, which I think is a compliment. I wish there were more opportunities for this kind of thing!

Will good stained glass continue to exist? Has really good stained glass ever existed? The depressing answer to both questions is, "yes, but very little." Books on the subject are listed in booksellers' catalogues among "the minor arts." The art is minor when it is mediocre: when it is first class it is major, like any other art. But major or minor, it *always* involves a craft as well, which is what the booksellers really mean.

Craft is in constant need of direction and control and nourishment of all kinds from art: from painting, sculpture, and architecture. It seldom gets it. When it does, fine stained glass can happen; when it doesn't, ordinary "commercial glass"—just another window—is added to the ghastly, vast, existing stock.

The average stained-glass designer-craftsman of our own day was apprenticed, when he was a beginner, to an artist-craftsman, or he was at an art school which had a stained-glass department. When young, in any case, he was in direct touch with art in some way, if only studying it "in the museum," as directed by Degas, or doing some life drawings in the evenings. If he is successful in his career however he cannot go on being in direct touch with art after a few years, unless he struggles hard in his spare time. He will be influenced, gradually and inevitably, by the job in hand, trimming his original gift. And he will probably be lost before he realizes his situation, for the "good" man is always in demand, and the money is useful. But, before he gets finally lost, if we search him out we find that he dare not get in touch with art again—the art he began to know as an apprentice or art student—because he would lose his acquired "vision," which is delivering the required goods. And if he lost that he would do the job that had come to be expected of him badly; he would be "experimenting," and looking for new ways of "seeing," and once he starts that he is no longer the good, ordinary man.

There is a gulf fixed between any craft and art. It can be leaped, but anyone leaping it must do so with a clear vision and a stout heart.

Stained glass is a great leader-astray for anyone who works at it— designer and craftsman alike. In terms of color and form, it is eccentric. Color is abnormally bright, since the light comes through the material instead of being reflected from the surface; tone is usually dictated by bounding leads or area joints of some kind. The whole thing is imprisoned within glazing bars that form an inexorable grid and are structurally necessary. This is its proper, splendid, discipline. But constant reference back to painting as a source and norm is essential—it is the staff of the glass-maker's life, however much this gets forgotten. The stained-glass studio can provide a marvelous life of communal work and camaraderie—and has clearly done so since the twelfth century—but the big problems of painting and sculpture are still best tackled in isolation. The undiluted practice of a craft purely as a craft prejudices even the most innocent eyes.

This situation bears on the whole history of stained glass. But, for the moment, think again of the position of our young craftsman, who has now emerged from the stained-glass department of his art school or apprenticeship in a studio, and has had a commission of his own. He has been drawing and painting in the life class or studying basic form and has some personal ideas about color and shape which need to crystallize and cohere. He is influenced by some admired painter or by some influential student, and his painting is forming itself in this way at the moment. In order to keep going, he seizes the job with enthusiasm. If he is exceptionally talented and lucky, he gets another. For the time being he has to do all the work himself, making as well as designing. The making—cutting, painting, firing, leading—is demanding, for it must be precise and is extremely time-consuming and pre-occupying. The craftsman has already begun to take over from the artist. If he still draws and paints, his vision will be influenced, however little, by practice of the craft. The way stained glass falls into "right" patterns in relation to lead lines—right for stained glass—influences vision and painting practice. If he does not keep the two things going side by side, or at least on equal terms, he is lost. His painting will cease and his stained glass will become stereotyped.

Herbert Read prophesied forty years ago that "the only hope of any reform would seem to lie in the final triumph of those principles for which William Morris stood. For these principles are not altogether dead: they have merely migrated, and on the continent, especially in Germany, there is a school of glass-painting which is not only modern in intention, but is inspired by all that is vital and significant in modern art." And he mentions Johan Thorn Prikker and Carl Schmidt-Rottluff, and Thorn Prikker's "fine modern glass" at Hagen railway station.[2]

There were signs before the Second World War, though they were pretty isolated signs, that modern art might really do more than nod occasionally at stained glass: that it might break in as it had broken into the theatre, especially the ballet, through Diaghilev. Sophie Taueber-Arp and Theo van Doesburg made windows related to the De Stijl and constructivist movements in the early 1920s. Joseph Albers made panels with fragments at the Bauhaus. Marcel Gromaire and other modern painters were designing windows when the war began. Evie Hone, who had studied with Léger and Gleizes, was at work in Ireland making painter's windows conceived in terms of glass. But it was not until the war ended that the modern revival really got on the move. The list of artist-interpreter, double-harness, designer-makers of the last twenty years is a long one. It includes Matisse/Paul Bony, Léger/Jean Barillet, Braque/Bony, and Chagall/Charles Marq.

New churches with money to spare, that is what are needed! Good artists can be trusted—so clergy, be bolder! Until you become so, I can only end as I began: there is good stained glass, but only a little. The great windows of modern times are all the work of artists working with collaborative craftsmen. They could be seen to represent an eleventh-hour rescue for a lowered and degraded medium with its back to the wall—held to ransom on the one hand by its own conscience in relation to art, on the other by the conservatism of patrons and the clergy. But, looking back over the whole performance for the past hundred years, it may be that the few great modern windows are more justly interpreted as the expected hillocks in a generally flat and dismal prospect. Such interest and excitement as they have is, anyway, a direct reflection of the interest and excitement of the art contemporary with them.

The windows by Matisse at Vence are the pure expression of a painter who thought deeply about the stained glass medium and used it for his own entirely honest ends. They are the kind of free adaptation of his very original late *papiers collés,* and are cut from clear, colored glass without any painted design or modification added; they are thought of as light-transmitting from the beginning. And the way their image is doubled on the floor of the chapel in sunshine is one of their prime beauties.

The Léger windows in the small suburban church at Audincourt (a suburb of Montbeliard, where Peugeot cars are made) are masterpieces of a different kind, symbolic and heraldic; designed by a man of such conviction and strength that they are, as it were, "signed all over." And this is in spite of the fact that they were executed by another man (Jean Barillet) in that most difficult medium, *dalle de verre* —especially difficult on this rather small scale where every piece of glass bonded in concrete counts in the total effect.

These two examples deny every precept laid down for the medium, in principle or practice, before they happened, just as Picasso's designs for *Tricorne* disobeyed all the stage design rules in 1919. It was aggressively simple, unmysterious, and self-assertive. By themselves, they have opened up infinite possibilities, though it is most unlikely that these possibilities will be pursued and developed. Nobody can move the body of stained glass practice and expertise at a faster rate than it wishes to be moved; and it is the servant of a very slow-moving tradition. It is the traction engine of the crafts.

Now that we have a window by Marc Chagall in England, at Tudely, near Tonbridge in Kent, his message may become more real and urgent, and acceptable. Chagall himself paints on the glass. Charles Marq, his collaborator, obviously has a strong influence in many ways —on the choice of glass, placing of leads and so on—but Chagall's technique makes a convincing over-all statement. He works with an adaption and not a repetition of his painting technique, and the windows he produces are a real contribution to the medium, not a mere extension of painting.

TWENTIETH-CENTURY STAINED GLASS

MARTIN HARRISON

Having for more than ten years studied the history of stained glass, I have reached a point where I feel it is doubtful that what the medium of stained glass needs right now is yet another view of its history: that is to say, it already has a record, for two centuries at least, of having been dangerously preoccupied with the past. This tendency to retreat into historicism, together with too great a fascination with craft and technique for their own sakes, seems to have bedevilled the art of stained glass in recent times.

Conscious that a large proportion of those who read this book will be American, it is best I lay my cards on the table right away. From where I stand, Neo-Tiffany, post-pop, hyperrealist, and rehashed German work just will not do any longer: flashed rubies and a vegetarian diet are no substitute for works which are determined to explore new possibilities in a medium which is surely capable of being stretched much more than hitherto. The majority of those making stained glass in the USA (and many, of course, elsewhere) appear to be young (under forty years old): they seem to suffer from a surfeit of 1960s-generated hippie/mystical/Zen/nice-liberal/comfy craft apathy. But it was with the hope that a few of them might share my optimism that some 1970s/1980s energy and ideas could infuse the medium, that I embarked on writing this chapter. Not that I believe no stained glass of real significance is being designed at this moment. To declare, at this point, my affiliations: I believe that two greatly contrasting personalities, Johannes Schreiter in Germany and Brian Clarke in England, are both producing work of an undeniably architectural nature, and yet of a subtlety which ranks it as "Art" outside of the narrower context of being simply stained glass. My intention is to examine their work a little more closely later, but first I want to try and indicate some of the more significant events in modern stained-glass history, in the hope that this might help to make the present position, and future possibilities, a little clearer.

The Glass Pavilion, Werkbund Exhibition, Cologne, 1914

Any attempt at an appraisal of the recent history of stained glass would be wasted were it not to recognize the most urgent present need: that architects and others who commission new buildings must be shocked into an awareness of the real and continuing potential of stained glass as a unique architectural medium for introducing light and color. The value of color in architecture is becoming increasingly recognized in certain quarters—for example, in the work of certain postmodern and high technology architects—but, in identifying some precedents for the imaginative architectural use of stained glass, I want to show how, in the twentieth century, the opportunity to restore it to the position of a really vital and integral architectural medium was largely lost; and I further aim to suggest that this might still be a realistic achievement.

Glass itself has played a central role in the development of modern architecture, from Fontaine's Galerie d'Orleans of 1829 through to S.O.M.'s Lever House and Mies van der Rohe's Seagram Building in the 1950s in New York. Though glass has become one of the principal building materials identified with the modern movement in architecture, its use as the main element of a futurist(ic) Crystal City was originally part of the vision of the Berlin expressionists, particularly Paul Scheerbart, Bruno Taut, and Arthur Korn. Scheerbart, better known as a poet and author of mystical novels, wrote *Glasarchitektur* in 1914, the year before his death. Taut's famous Glass Pavilion, made for the Cologne Werkbund Exhibition also in 1914, was dedicated to Scheerbart, who in turn dedicated to it the prophetic motto:

> Glass brings us the new age
> Brick culture does us only harm.

If all this seemed to augur well for glass, the promise was not truly fulfilled in architecture until the advent of the Lever House and Seagram Building, and in *stained* glass the promise was hardly fulfilled at all. I have linked the two together because the brighter future for stained glass must lie in its being inextricable from architecture; for too long, lip service has been paid to the concept of stained glass as an architectural medium, without firm evidence of a belief in the essential truth of that statement being shown either by architect or stained-glass designer.

A chief stumbling block has been that for many people stained glass is synonymous with ecclesiastical building. This was perhaps understandable, primarily because the first great era of stained glass was as a vital element of the great medieval cathedrals of Europe. It is instructive to note, however, how often the stained glass of the great cathedrals such as Chartres and Canterbury is still interpreted as a simple form of biblical instruction for the masses—who were presumably not usually equipped at that time with binoculars nor telephoto lenses—while its crucial architectural function as a modifier and subduer of light receives far less attention. With so little new church building in most parts of the world today, it is inevitable that the art of stained glass would die if the church were its only life-source; therefore it must be more widely utilized in secular building if it is to grow.

The other main problem is that there has been a negligible amount of cooperation between architect and stained-glass designer on a *scale* which might have allowed the opportunity for a truly impressive result. The outcome of this situation is all too clear in England at present where, ironically, at a time when the interest in stained glass is increasing all the time, the actual work being produced is trite and banal decoration—a sort of pale expressionism—of sickly-faced saints, straight off the nineteenth-century production line.

In the nineteenth century, the great majority of stained glass was usually limited by its being, for architects, little more than another weapon in the vocabulary of various style revivals of one kind or another. Occasionally, distinguished artists became involved in the medium, most notably Morris and Burne-Jones in England, and indeed, their collaboration sometimes did result in windows which lived up to expectations. This introduces what would seem to be today, not only for the practicing stained-glass artist, but for anyone who holds an opinion about the medium, the biggest bone of contention: that is the question, "Must a designer for stained glass also make his own windows?"

The involvement (or lack of it) of leading artists in stained glass is further illustrated in France. Earlier in the nineteenth century, Ingres, Delacroix, and Flandrin had all designed windows; but, with the possible exception of the symbolist painter Maurice Denis in the 1890s, the link is broken until the revival of interest in the 1930s, which resulted in the now famous collaborations between craftsmen and such artists as Matisse, Léger, Rouault, Manessier, Bazaine, Braque, and Chagall. (One development in the interim, though not to be a prominent milestone in stained-glass history, deserves mention here. Auguste Perret, the architect renowned for his pioneering use of reinforced concrete at the beginning of the century in his churches of Notre Dame at le Raincy (1922–23) and St. Theresa at Montmagny (1925), utilized the concrete to enable him to provide vast "window walls," though the result resembles more a muscular plain glazing than anything that could be defined as stained glass.)

In England at the turn of the century, the most interesting stained glass was being done by the Arts & Crafts school, whose unofficial leader was Christopher Whall (1849–1924). His belief in a craft-oriented studio democratically organized under master and apprentice lines was in the spirit of William Morris (and ultimately Ruskin)—derived Socialism. Their concept of a workforce (including the designer) trained to be competent in all stages of stained-glass production was a reaction against the more extreme factory-like, mass-production methods of the large Victorian studios. Insofar as these methods had led to largely stereotyped and unsatisfactory products, the revolt was justified and, indeed, successfully resulted in a much fresher and more committed approach. The problem in England (and it would appear to be true of the USA also) has been that the Arts & Crafts dictum perpetuated long after its useful life was over, and is still applied as a *sine qua non* of good stained glass. However, it would seem to be true as a matter of historical fact, that very few of the great designs for stained glass have come from those who have spent too much time contemplating which sort of kiln to buy at the expense of original thought about what they might do with the medium.

No one would deny the necessity for fine craftsmanship. It is simply that the great designer and the great craftsman are usually psychologically and temperamentally different characters, and it is self-defeating to insist they must be one and the same person. The persistence of this attitude is surely one of the principal reasons for England and the USA today remaining primarily a backwater of the art of stained glass.

Attempts in England to produce stained glass which looked as though it actually belonged to the twentieth century were almost non-existent until John Piper's (b. 1903) belated first commission in 1955 (for the upper apse windows of Oundle School Chapel, Northants., England). Prior to that there were a few minor examples of semi-abstract glass from Roger Fry's Omega Workshops (c. 1914) and one completely abstract set by Alfred Wolmark (1877–1961) in the west windows of St. Mary's Church, Slough, Bucks., England (1915–1917). Wolmark was a painter associated with the vorticist movement, and the windows are made of small irregular pieces of bright primary-colored glass. They became the subject of a legal controversy in 1918 as to whether the artist "conformed to the instructions that the design was not to contain any saints or haloes or anything of that kind." The question for the court was: "whether that condition was fulfilled by a window which was described by Mr. Compton, K.C., as representing Adam and Eve in the Garden of Eden!" Mr. Justice Darling could not see any meaning in it and the whole affair was evidently more than the British public could take, and the experiment never repeated.

It is most surprising that there has so far been nobody willing in the history of twentieth century stained glass to champion its pioneers. Everyone has, for example, heard of the Bauhaus, but many still register shock on learning that the renowned art school included a flourishing stained-glass department. In fact, besides Sophie Taueber-Arp and Theo van Doesburg, both Paul Klee and Josef Albers were at some time involved with stained glass there. Similarly, no one has yet satisfactorily described the developments in modern stained glass. This absence of any generally accepted common background makes it all the more difficult to analyze current investigations in the medium. Nevertheless, I shall attempt to at least suggest an outline for future studies of this topic.

The twentieth century opened in a spirit of fervent reaction by the artistic avant-garde against the backward-looking decadence of the time. Already the relationship between "fine art" and stained glass had become far more complex than hitherto. In the nineteenth century, the Pre-Raphaelite movement in art, the Anglo-Japanese style, and symbolism were all closely parallelled in stained glass, but the work of the impressionists—especially that of the "softer focus" exponents such as Monet and Renoir—would clearly never translate easily into stained glass. From this point on, just as art started to leave many of its old public behind when it became less preoccupied with physical reality, so a split occurred between many stained-glass designers and avant-garde artists. The links with progressive architecture were more closely maintained, however.

In Glasgow during the 1890s, Charles Rennie Mackintosh (1868–1928), now justly renowned as a pioneer of the modern movement, became the leader of a group of young designers and architects. He built only one church (Queen's Cross Church, Glasgow, 1896—now the headquarters of the Charles Rennie Mackintosh Society), and the small amount of colored glass in it is of little significance though for his secular buildings, such as the Willow Tea Rooms in Glasgow he designed some fine near-abstract glass and opalescent panels. His influence on the Vienna secessionists has been acknowledged however, and seems to have been particularly strong on Koloman Moser (1868–1918), whose stained glass was of a kind one imagines would have given much satisfaction to Mackintosh. Moser's window at the Steinhof Church, Vienna (1907) places simplified hieratic figures on a background which anticipates geometrical abstraction, much akin to the architect's own later, more rectilinear work.

C. R. Mackintosh: Willow Tea Rooms,
Glasgow, 1904 (60 × 19 cm.)

There is a strong parallel between Mackintosh in Scotland and Frank Lloyd Wright (1869–1959) in the USA. Wright, too, was a profoundly influential architect and, like Mackintosh, was very fond of using stained glass in his houses. Other distinguished designers associated with Art Nouveau dabbled in stained glass, among them Alphonse Mucha (Prague Cathedral), Jan Toorop, Louis Tiffany, Melchior Lechter, and Henry van de Velde. Van de Velde was in the forefront of the architectural debate in Europe at the beginning of the twentieth century (a central figure in the setting up of the Weimar School of Applied Arts in 1906, which formed the basis for the later Weimar Bauhaus). Both he and Peter Behrens, himself, of course, a major architect, designed for stained glass, though in neither case did the results aspire to more than a rather florid, if attractive, art-nouveau pattern-work.

Nevertheless, it was in Germany that much of the finest twentieth-century stained glass was to happen. Most prominent in the first three decades was Johan Thorn Prikker (1868–1932). He has received some recognition over the last ten years for his early work as a symbolist painter, but his stained glass is still grossly neglected. He is, in my opinion, a figure crucial to the thorough understanding of the modern development of stained glass, and an English-language study of his work is long overdue. Besides stained glass, he also designed many textiles and mosaics and this, coupled with his early paintings, should have been enough to ensure for him a more prominent place in twentieth-century art history.

He arrived in Germany from his native Holland in 1904. During his life he taught at Köln, Düsseldorf, Krefeld, and Essen, and became friendly with a circle which included Van de Velde, Olbrich, and Behrens. His earliest stained glass was mostly figurative, of a strongly symbolist kind. It became increasingly expressionist in character toward the outbreak of the First World War—indeed, Thorn Prikker was in close touch with the *Blaue Reiter* group at this time. By 1921, he had completely rejected the figurative element from his work as being irrelevant and began designing in a cool and geometrical abstract style, clearly influenced by De Stijl theory and showing he must have been well aware of the ideas promoted by the Bauhaus. During the 1920s, his abstract work fluctuated, sometimes approaching a jazz or art deco restlessness and eclecticism, but he produced, towards the end of the decade a stream of masterpieces, culminating in the panel

Orange a stunningly economical and radically simplified work of 1931—one which astonishingly anticipates many later developments. Other prominent artists have designed for stained glass in this century, but Thorn Prikker is unique in that he worked with the medium for thirty years, during which time it remained the dominant aspect of his *oeuvre*. Ironically, the only critical appreciation Thorn Prikker received outside of Germany was in *English Stained Glass,* by the perceptive Herbert Read, where he refers to the "Fine modern glass . . ." at Hagen railway station (actually dating from 1911 and made by Gottfreid Heinersdorf).[1] It is to be hoped that Thorn Prikker will soon receive the recognition due to him.

Other artists in Germany at this time, designing for stained glass, were, for example, Cesar Klein, Karl Schmidt-Rottluff, and Heinrich Campendonk, but their efforts, while certainly spirited in comparison with the enfeebled and diluted Gothic of their English and American counterparts, were rather less refined than those of their more capable fellow countrymen. The work of all three was mostly figurative, and this was bound to pose problems by the 1920s, however devout the exponent. A comparison could be drawn with the work of two Irish-born ladies: Wilhelmina Geddes and Evie Hone. The early work of both was sometimes quite outstanding (Miss Geddes' east window in St. Luke's, Wallsend-on-Tyne, Northumberland, England, of 1922, is especially deserving of mention) but, while their sincerity cannot be questioned, the desire to introduce expressive power into their work often resulted in the merely crude. At the opposite extreme it is a cause for regret that so little Bauhaus glass has survived. There are, however, a few van Doesburg panels in private hands in Europe, and the McCrory Corporation Collection in New York includes a small, but remarkable, Albers panel which employs the "window as screen" concept he used in the windows for Gropius' house for Dr. Sommerfeld at Berlin-Dahlem (1922), and Dr. Otte's House at Berlin-Zehlendorf (1922–23). No doubt further research will bring other examples to light.

Like Campendonk, Anton Wendling (1891–1965) was a pupil of Thorn Prikker and he was responsible, together with Georg Meistermann (b. 1911) for the most innovative German stained glass between 1935 and 1955 (their contributions and more recent German work is admirably elucidated by M. Coulon-Rigaud in his essay). Meistermann is still designing stained glass, and together with Ludwig Schaffrath (b. 1924) and Johannes Schreiter (b. 1930), is the most acclaimed of

Wilhelmina Geddes: East Window of St. Lukes,
Wallsend-on-Tyne, Northumberland, 1922

Johan Thorn-Prikker: ''Orange,'' 1931
(49 × 39 cm.)

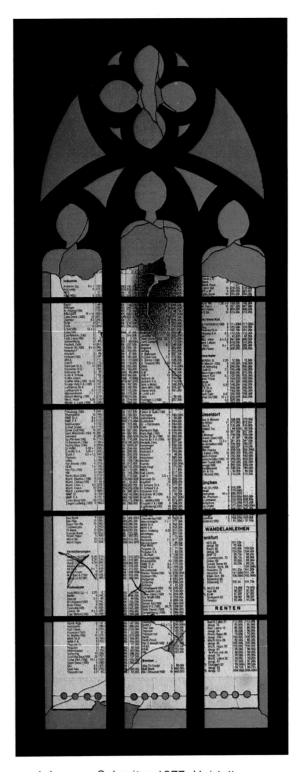

Johannes Schreiter 1977, Heidelberg.
One of a series of textual window designs,
this one containing a section of recent stock market ratings.

Brian Clarke: Design for 1000 sq. ft. window in the entrance to Thorn
House, Headquarters of Thorn Electrical Industries, London, 1978
Architects: Sir Basil Spence and Partners

TWENTIETH-CENTURY STAINED GLASS

Piano and Rogers
Centre Pompidou, Paris, 1977

the post-war Germans. Schaffrath is the only one of these artists for whom we have a monograph so far,[2] and it is imperative that the others soon receive similar treatment.

In 1973 I asked the architect James Stirling if, since he had never used stained glass in any of his buildings, he had a particular aversion to the medium. He replied that this was not the case, rather that he had simply never seen any modern stained glass he would consider using. When an outstanding architect makes such a statement it is surely time for the stained-glass fraternity to prick up their ears and take note. For, though one would hope that if Stirling and the few others of his stature could see the best new work they might be persuaded to reconsider, one can only sympathize with his opinion. It was his remark which originally fired me to seek out what current work in stained glass might be deserving of being afforded exciting architectural opportunities.

In the most recent work of Johannes Schreiter and Brian Clarke, I believe that stained glass has at last reached that point. Both are deeply committed artists with an existence both within and without glass art. Both are unswervingly devoted to the concept of "art for architecture," but what they have, in their very different ways, succeeded in doing in their latest works, is to narrow down the gap between their art and their stained glass, so that the two are evolving side by side. Previously, it seemed that the compromises involved in adapting stained glass to specific architectural situations resulted in a dilution of these artists' very strongest messages; but, with Schreiter's series for Heidelberg and Brian Clarke's design for a London office window any hint of compromise is banished, and again we have architectural stained glass that ranks as serious investigative art. Besides its extraordinary linear qualities, Schreiter's Heidelberg design incorporates Brandcollage elements and references to the Stock Exchange from his recent graphics—in terms of content, an unprecedented step; and Clarke's design contains diverse allusions ranging through constructivism, electronics, and Post–New-Wave music.

Earlier in this essay I referred to Christopher Whall as the leader of the Arts & Crafts movement in stained glass in Britain. In 1896, he produced a paper in conjunction with Halsey Ricardo entitled, "The Architect's Use of Colour."[3] In 1906, Ricardo built a house in Addison Road, Kensington, London, faced entirely in blue, green and white glazed tiles. However, the use of color in architecture has rarely received more than superficial attention until recently, with the work of, for example, the industrial buildings by the Urbane Group, Piano & Rogers, Corsini & Wiskemann, and Foster Associates. Surely, here again, was a lost opportunity for stained glass; but equally surely the opportunity must be present in the future for the situation to be remedied—at least in a secular context. Any efforts to establish stained glass as "art" by spurious attempts at mimicry of bourgeois easel art to be sold in galleries must ultimately meet with the fate it deserves. Only when the would-be designer of stained glass has integrated the "art" into his own philosophy and approach will the end result transcend the limited artsy-craftsy horizons of the great majority of recent stained glass and fulfill the promise of stained glass as an architectural medium of the future.

PORTFOLIO

Johannes Schreiter

Johannes Schreiter was born in 1930 in Bucholz/Erzgebirge. In 1948 he studied at Abitur, and from 1946–1957 he studied in Munster, Mainz and Berlin. In 1958 he received the Friedrich-Ebert-Stiftung stipendium for the invention of fusion-collage. He was awarded the Gold Medal in the second National Biennale for Christian Art in Salzburg in 1960, and from then until 1963 he was Director of a division in the School of Art in Bremen. In that same year he became a professor in the city high school for Decorative Arts, Frankfurt. In 1970 Mr. Schreiter made the first of the "smoked body" pictures; these led, in 1972, to a series of so-called "fragment" pictures. In his aquatints Schreiter changed the "smoked body" into fantastic "organisms" which often took on animalistic traits. In 1974 Mr. Schreiter was a prize winner at the Exhibition of European Graphic Art of the Future, and in 1977 he received the Phillip Morris Prize. Since 1960, Schreiter has been particularly concerned with architectural art. He has made internationally esteemed windows for historical and contemporary buildings. Although as an artist he is passionately independent, he belongs to the West German Künstlerbund, and to the Neuen Darmstadt Secession. His works may be found in numerous museums, both in Germany and other countries.

His projects include: St. Margaret's, Burgstadt/Main; Church of the Holy Spirit, Bremen-Neue Vahr; Johannesbund, Leutesdorf/Rhein; St. John's Church, Bremerhaven-Lehe; St. Michael's Church (choir window), Bremerhaven; St. Marien's, Gottingen; Protestant Church, Oberkirch/Baden; Protestant Church, Laufenburg/ bei Sackingen; Munster (Chapel of the Sacrament), Essen; Festeburg-Kirche, Frankfurt-Main; St. Marien's, Dortmund; Catholic Church and Youth Center, Weibern/Eifel; Cemetery Church, Endenburg/ Schwarzwald; St. Bonifatius', Hofheim/Taunus.

JOHANNES SCHREITER

Brandcollage, "Waiting for Godot," City Collection, Darmstadt, 1966

JOHANNES SCHREITER

Detail Brandcollage, 1972
(24.3 × 18.5 cm.) (Meerwein Collection, *Mainz*)

JOHANNES SCHREITER

Detail Serigraphie (60 × 44.7 cm.), 1974

JOHANNES SCHREITER

Exterior view of choir windows in the chapel of
the Exerzitienhaus, Johannesbund, Leutesdorf/Rhein, 1966

JOHANNES SCHREITER

Window in the village church, Endenburg,
Black Forest, 1971 (188 × 107 cm.)

JOHANNES SCHREITER

West Window at St. Marien, Dortmund, 1972
(1007 × 375 cm.)

JOHANNES SCHREITER

Exterior view of Festeburg church, Frankfurt, 1968, concrete and
slab glass. Architects: Römer and Baùmgart

JOHANNES SCHREITER

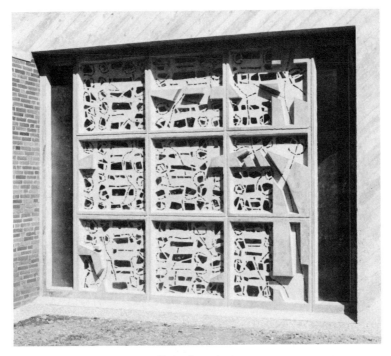

Exterior view

Interior view

JOHANNES SCHREITER

Window in St. Marien, Dortmund, 1971 (318 × 205 cm.)

JOHANNES SCHREITER

Window in St. Marien, Dortmund, 1971 (186 × 62 cm.)

JOHANNES SCHREITER

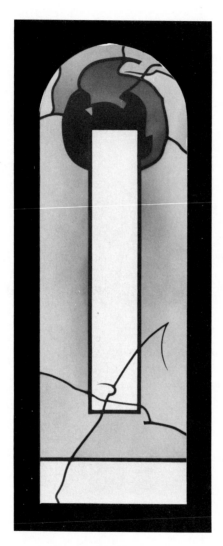 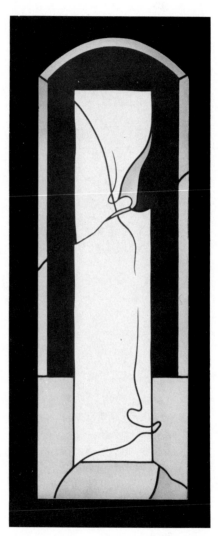

Model
Window in the Romanesque Basilica,
St. Lubentius, Dietkirchen, 1975
(121 × 39 cm.)

Alternative design for
St. Lubentius, Dietkirchen, 1975

JOHANNES SCHREITER

Interior view of choir windows in the chapel of
the Exerzitienhaus, Johannesbund, Leutesdorf/Rhein

Six south windows in the Catholic Church
St. Ansgar, Södertälje Sweden, 1976. Architect: Fritz Voigt
Executed by W. Derix, Glasgestaltung, Rottweil and Taunusstein

JOHANNES SCHREITER

Detail of the north apse window in the Catholic Church at
St. Laurentius, Niederkalbach bei Fulda, 1977 (256 × 80 cm.)
Executed by W. Derix, Taunusstein

JOHANNES SCHREITER

Model Designs,
North Choir Windows for Notre Dame, Douai, France, 1976

JOHANNES SCHREITER

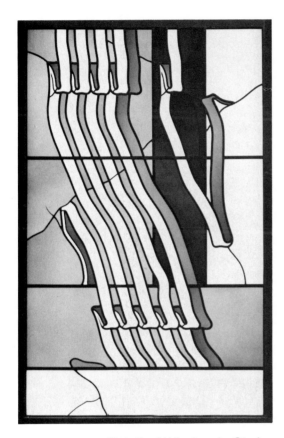

Detail of Window in St. Ansgar's, Södertälje, Sweden, 1975
(Six windows in all: 526 × 103 cm.; detail 167 × 103 cm.)

JOHANNES SCHREITER

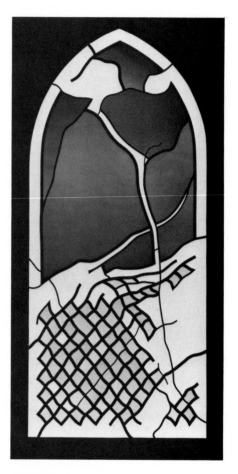

Left window in the
south aisle of the Munsterkirche,
St. Bonifatius, Hameln, 1977
(131 × 58 cm.) Opaque Antique glass & perspex
Executed by W. Derix, Taunusstein

JOHANNES SCHREITER

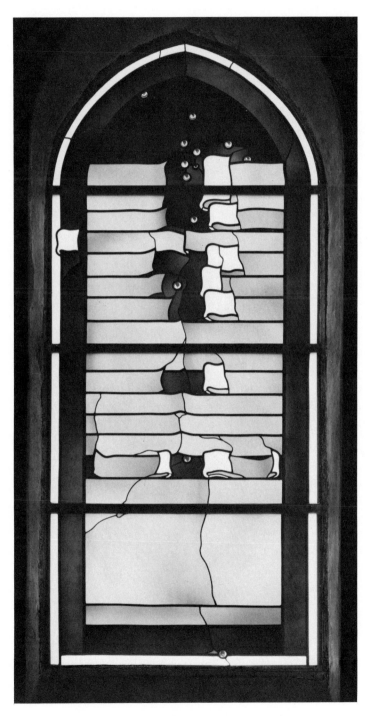

Window in the Sacraments Chapel in
Limbourg Cathedral, 1977 (284 × 123 cm.)

JOHANNES SCHREITER

Right window in the south aisle. Some of the eastern choir
windows in the Church of Notre Dame, Douai, France (850 cm. × 168 cm.)
Designed 1975–77 Executed by W. Derix, Taunusstein

Joachim Edgar Klos

Klos was born November 16, 1931, in Weidar, Thüringen. During the years 1947–49, he studied at the State University for Architecture and Fine Arts in Weimar. In 1951 the University closed down the Department of Fine Arts. His studies ended, he moved to the Federal Republic of Germany via Berlin. He studied at the Art School, Krefeld, until 1957, specializing in mosaic and glass painting. Here he met the artist, Carola Stammen. They were married in 1955 and settled in Münchengladbach. Two years later, when he finished his studies, Klos passed the state examinations, and began working as an independent painter and graphic artist with great success.

He shared with Professor Georg Meistermann the prize given by the Glashutte Mittinger & Co., Darmstadt, for the best glass painting of 1959. Numerous exhibits followed with acquisitions of his works by museums in Europe and South America.

In 1968 he built his home and studio in Schaag, Nettetal, where he lives with his wife and six children.

St. Nikolaus, Walbeck, 1968 (detail)

Liebfrauen, Bocholt, 1969

St. Adelheid, Geldern, 1957

JOACHIM KLOS

St. Adelheid, Geldern, 1967 (250 sq. m.)

Ludwig Schaffrath

MARTIN HARRISON

Ludwig Schaffrath was born in 1924 in Alsdorf, near Aachen, West Germany. From 1945 to 1946 he studied at the Schluterschule, and from 1946 to 1953 he was assistant to Professor Wendling, Architecture Department, Aachen Technical College. Since 1954 he has worked in Alsdorf-Ofden.

Examples of his work in glass and mosaic can be found in over one hundred and fifty churches, schools, hospitals and other public institutions, including the following: Aachen Cathedral Cloisters; St. Josef's, Aachen; Alsdorf Townhall (mosaics); St. Marien's, Bad Zwischenahn; St. Marien's, Bockorst; St. Johannes', Dortmund-Kurl; St. Antonius Hospital, Eschweiler (mosaics and chapel windows); St. Martin's, Hagen-Kabel; Christi Gebert, Köln-Mengenich; Papst-Johannes-Haus, Krefeld (chapel windows); St. Martin's, Schwalbach Limes; St. Michael's, Schweinfurt; St. Johannes', Tennenbronn; and Würzburg Cathedral.

Exterior view of the entrance wall,
design of windows and concrete facade,
Geilenkirchen-Bauchum St. Josef, 1974
Architect: Matthias Kleuters

Opposite: Windows of the entrance wall (detail)

Exterior view of a window,
Nativity, Köln-Mengenich, 1977

Schwalbach-Limes, St. Martin, 1973–74

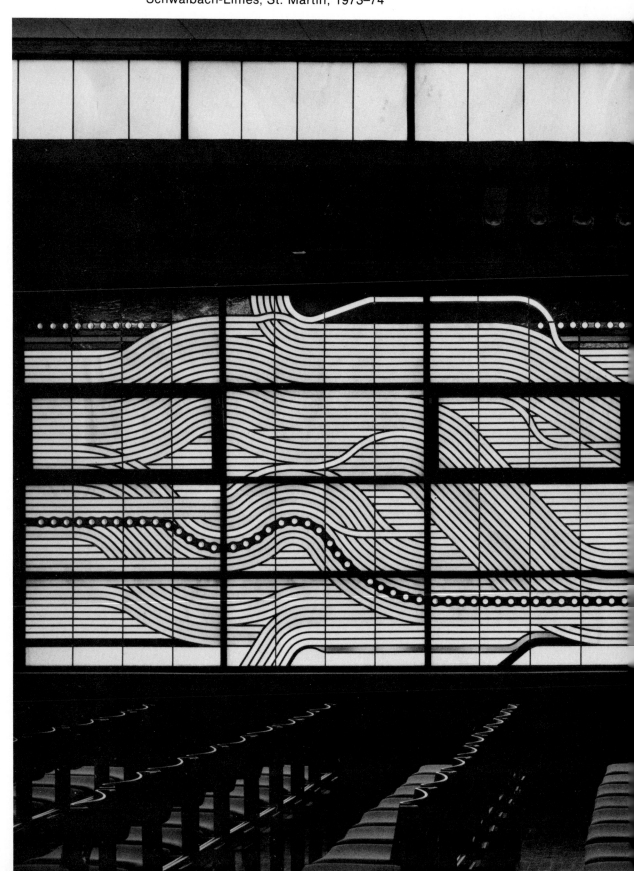

LUDWIG SCHAFFRATH

Exterior view of the cloister windows, Aachen Cathedral, 1964–65

LUDWIG SCHAFFRATH

One of a series of six windows for the Chapel,
St. Antonius Hospital, Eschweiler, West Germany, 1976

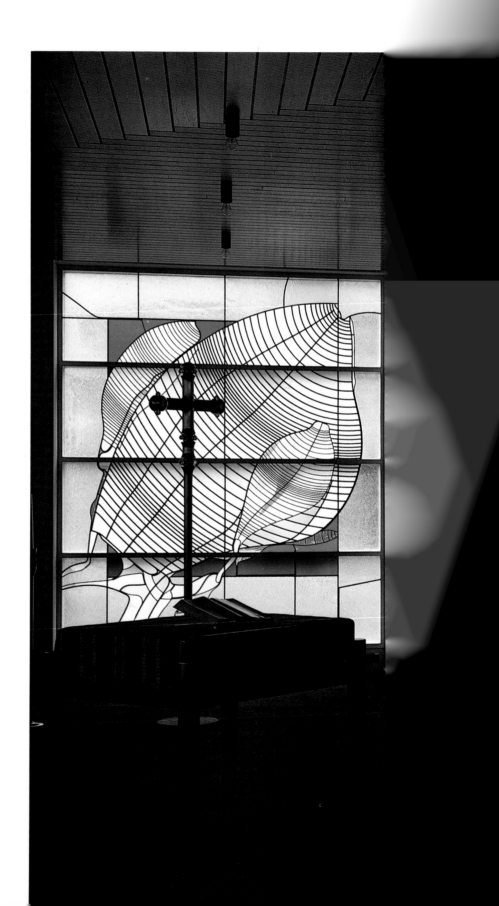

LUDWIG SCHAFFRATH

Windows for the Chapel, St. Antonius Hospital, Eschweiler, West Germany, 1976

LUDWIG SCHAFFRATH

Exterior view of the entrance hall window, Swimming Pool,
Ubach-Palenberg, 1973

LUDWIG SCHAFFRATH

Exterior view of the east wall with lit interior

Window in the workday chapel, Bad Zwischenahn/St. Marien, 1970–71

Wilhelm Buschulte

DR. H. OIDTMANN

Wilhelm Buschulte was born in Massen, near Unna in 1923. He attended the Akademie fur Bildende, Kunste in Munich.

Among his many stained-glass works are windows included in: St. Folian's, Essen (Munsterkirche), Aachen; a Seminary in Cologne; a Catholic Church in Lonne bei Linger; Ratzeburge Cathedral; St. Francis's of Osnabruck; the Maria-Konigin of Saarbrucken; the Catholic Academy in Schwerte; and the Reformation Remembrance Church in Worms.

WILHELM BUSCHULTE

Nave Window in St. Paulus, Lovenich, 1973

WILHELM BUSCHULTE

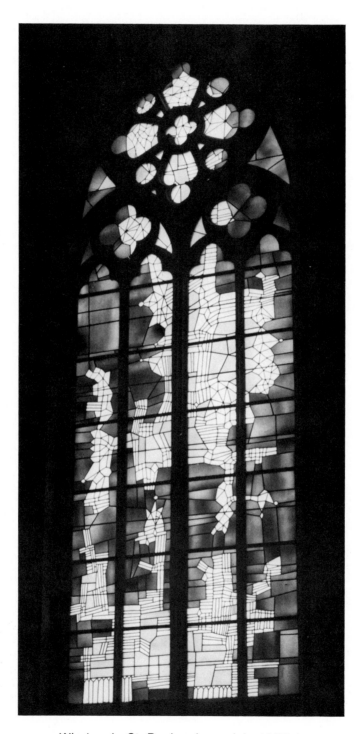

Window in St. Paulus, Lovenich, 1957

WILHELM BUSCHULTE

Window in St. Folian, Aachen, 1960

WILHELM BUSCHULTE

Window in Essen Münster, 1965

WILHELM BUSCHULTE

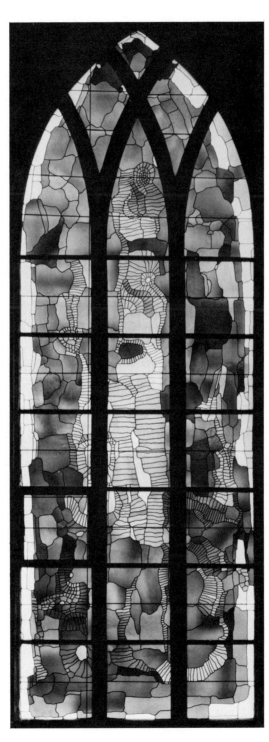

Window in Essen Münster, 1965

WILHELM BUSCHULTE

Window in the Church of the Holy Family, Oberhausen, 1958

WILHELM BUSCHULTE

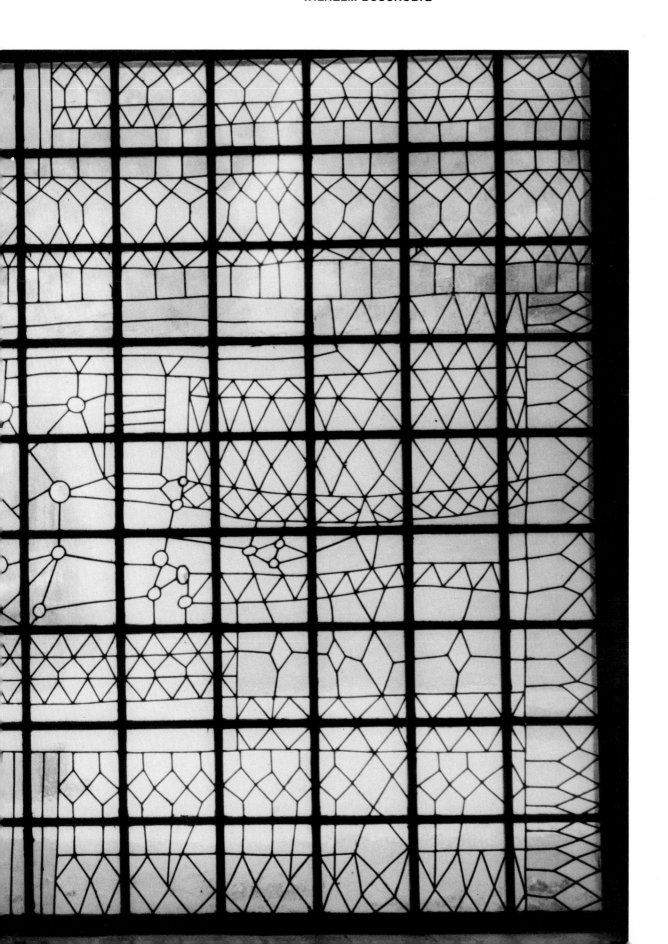

WILHELM BUSCHULTE

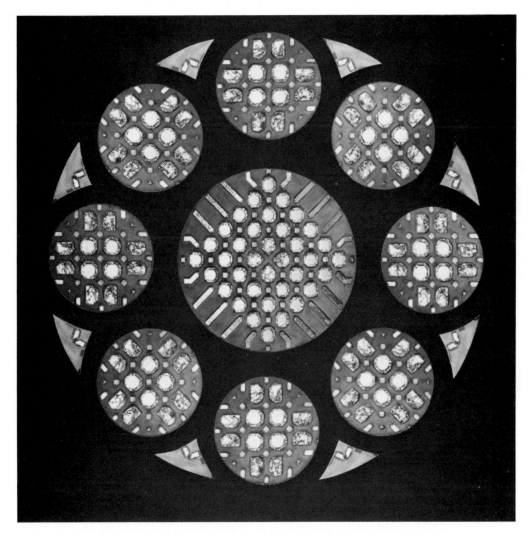

Rosette in the west gable of the Ratzeburge Dom, 1969
Steel, leaded on both sides, glazed with 45 mm.-thick Boussoisglass

Opposite: Window in St. Martinus, Linnich, 1969

Jochem Poensgen

Jochem Poensgen was born in 1931 in Düsseldorf. He is completely self-taught, and his works have been exhibited in such places as Munich, Düsseldorf, Paris, Darmstadt, Bombay, Rio de Janeiro, São Paolo, Belo Horizonte, and Wiesbaden, and London. Mr. Poensgen's graphic works include illustrations for *Die Zeit, Die Welt,* and *Spektrum.*

JOCHEM POENSGEN

Detail of window in the Chapel of St. Marien Hospital,
Ahaus/Westphalia, 1976

Exterior view of St. Elizabeth's Church, Bensberg-Refrath, 1962
(sculptured concrete and slab glass) Architect: Rotterdam Bensberg

Exterior view of Christ Church, Dinslaken, Niederrhein, 1967
Architect: Zelger & Zelger, Innsbruck and Essen

Interior detail of St. Elizabeth's Church, Bensberg-Refrath, 1962

Window in the Catholic Church
in Dundenheim near Offenburg/Baden, 1977

JOCHEM POENSGEN

Exhibition Window for Hein Derix Kevelaer, 1975 (161 × 161 cm.)

JOCHEM POENSGEN

Window in St. Martin's, Bad Honnef-Selhof, 1968
Architect: Wolfgarten Bad-Honnef

JOCHEM POENSGEN

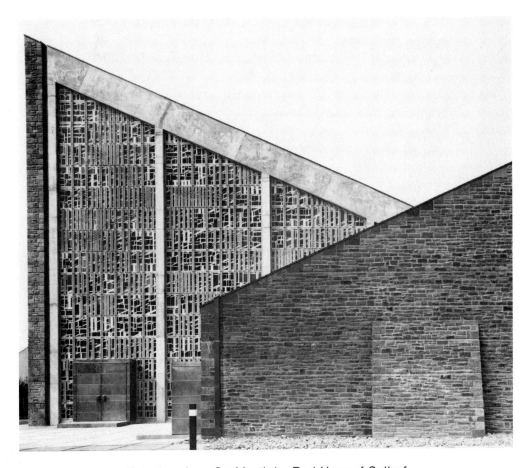

Exterior view, St. Martin's, Bad Honnef-Selhof

Overleaf: Windows in the parish church, Bleibach, 1977
(industrial glass and asbestos)

JOCHEM POENSGEN

Windows in concrete in the Catholic church of
St. Paulus, Konigsfeld, Black Forest, 1973

JOCHEM POENSGEN

Exterior view of windows

Window in Chapel of Luisenheims, Düsseldorf-Eller, 1971

Georg Meistermann

Georg Meistermann was born July 16, 1911, in Solingen. From 1932–33, he studied at the Academy of Fine Art in Düsseldorf under Heinrich Nauen and Ewald Matare, at which time his studies were broken off and he was forbidden to exhibit. In 1938, his first stained-glass window was executed for St. Engelbert in Solingen, which was later destroyed in the war, as were, in 1944, his early paintings. In 1945, his first exhibit was held in the Municipal Museum of Wuppertal. He received the Blevin-Devin Prize, Munich, in 1950, and the Municipal Prize for Culture, Wuppertal, in 1951. In 1952, while a visiting lecturer in Hamburg, Meistermann obtained a professorship at the Städelschule, Frankfurt-Main, and received the Municipal Prize for Culture in Köln. While a professor at the Academy for Art in Düsseldorf in 1955, he received the Grand Prize for Art from the State, Nordrhein-Westfalen. Other prizes he has received include the Prize for Glass Painting in both Darmstadt and Salzburg (1956 and 1958 respectively), the Distinguished Service Medal of the Federal Republic of Germany (1959), the Prize for Culture from the city of Solingen (1974), and the Government Prize from the State of Rheinland-Pfalz for art applied in architecture (1976). Except for a two-year period from 1965 to 1967 when he held a professorship at the Academy for Fine Arts in Munich, Meistermann was a professor at the Academy of Art in Karlsruhe from 1960 to 1976. From 1967 to 1972, he was President of the German Association of Artists. He currently resides in Cologne.

Window in the Parish Church, Bad-Kissingen, 1958–60

GEORG MEISTERMANN

St. Marien, Köln-Kalk, 1965

GEORG MEISTERMANN

Window in Bottrop Church entitled, "The Bottrop Spiral," 1959

GEORG MEISTERMANN

Window in the Cathedral, Würzburg, 1957

GEORG MEISTERMANN

Window in Deutscher Bank, Frankfurt, 1971

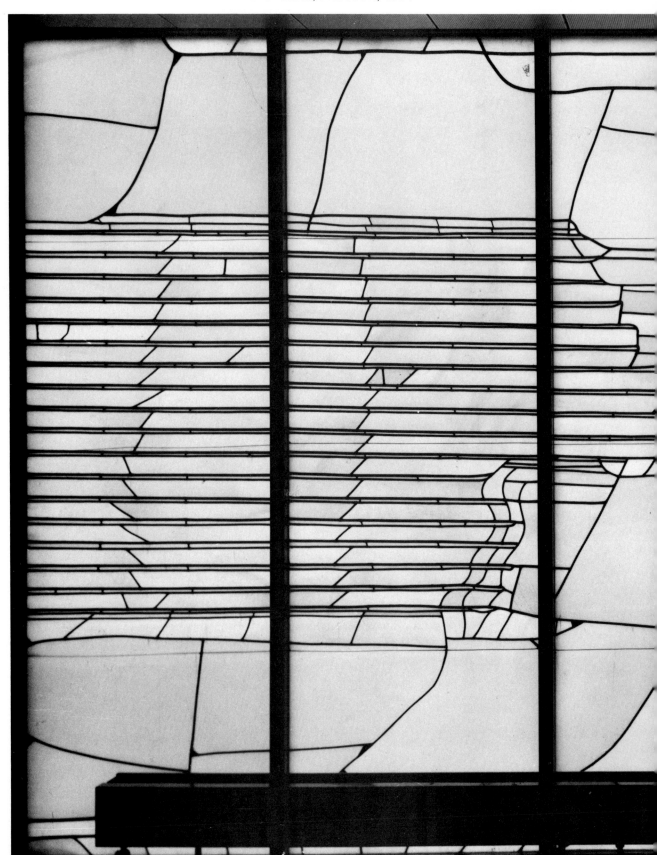

GEORG MEISTERMANN

GEORG MEISTERMANN

Choir windows in the Parish Church, Ottweiler/Saar, 1962

Brian Clarke

Brian Clarke was born in 1953 in Oldham, England and was educated at Oldham School of Art on a junior scholarship from eleven, Burnley College of Art, and the North Devon College. Since 1972 he has been working independently as a painter and stained-glass designer. In 1974 he became a Churchill Fellow in Paris, Rome, and West Germany, and in 1976 received the Churchill Extension Fellowship to the USA. The following year saw the first "new wave" paintings; and he was the subject of a B.B.C. documentary film in March 1979. Since 1978 he has been working in England and New York City, has had an exhibition of paintings at Sheffield City Polytechnic, and was a consultant with John Piper to the Festival of the City of London GLASS/LIGHT exhibition.

Selected projects include: Preston Guild Window, 1972; Longridge Parish Church, 1974 (20 windows); Thornton Cleveleys Parish Church, 1976 (10 windows); the first window derived from Japanese screen painting, 1975 (private collection, Longton); the east window of the Habergham Parish Church, Burnley, Lancashire, 1976; designs for West Roundels, Derby Cathedral, 1976 (unrealised); Lytham St. Anne's, 1976; Velarde's St. Gabriel, Blackburn, 1977; a series of 45 paintings and a stained-glass window for the University of Nottingham, 1976–77; external relief with neon for the University of London, 1977; and a design for window and electronic assemblage, Thorn Industries, central London, 1978.

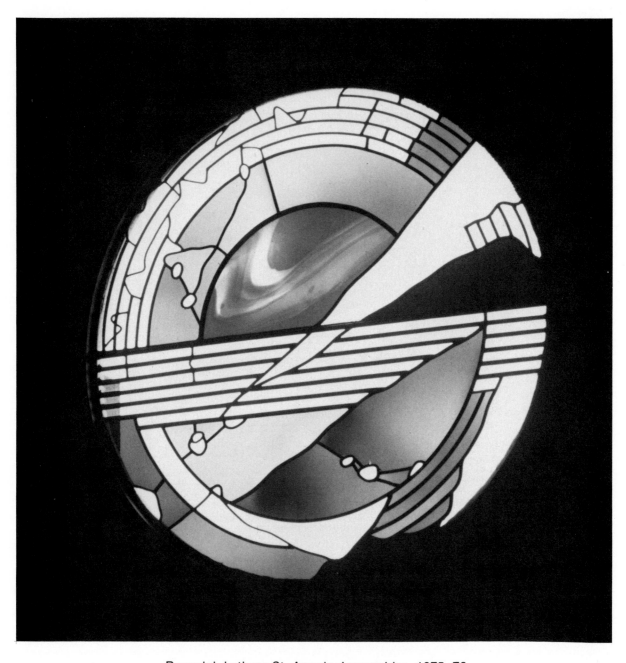

Roundel, Lytham St. Anne's, Lancashire, 1975–76

BRIAN CLARKE

Baptistery windows in St. Gabriel's Church, Blackburn, 1977
Architect: F. X. Velarde, 1932 (18 ft. × 1 ft.)

East window of Habergham Parish Church,
Burnley, Lancashire, 1976 (160 sq. ft.)

Design for south transept window in Luton Parish Church, 1977 (unrealized)

Window in private collection,
England, 1976–77

One of ten windows in
Thornton Parish Church, Lancashire,
1975–76 (total area: 250 sq. ft.)

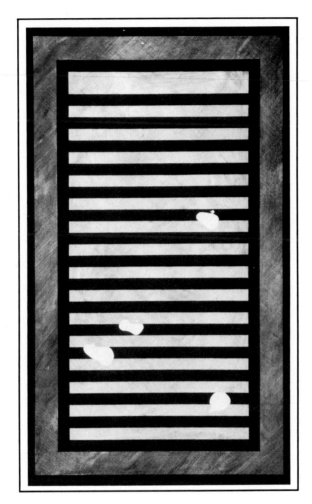

Painting in acrylic, 1977 (untitled)

BRIAN CLARKE

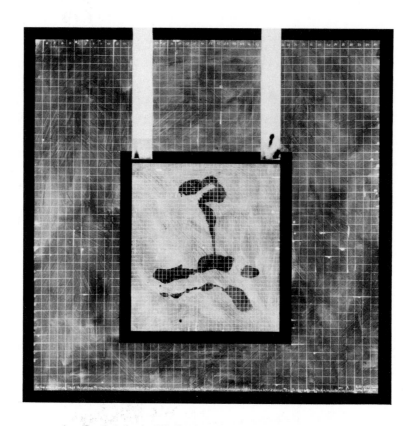

Le Corbusier's Right Angle, painting in acrylics
with applied singed canvas containing
quote from Le Corbusier's "Poem to the Right Angle," 1977

One of ten windows in Thornton Parish Church,
Lancashire, 1975–76 (total area: 250 sq. ft.)

BRIAN CLARKE

One of three two-light windows in
Birchover Parish Church, Derbyshire, England, 1977

BRIAN CLARKE

Window in private collection, England, 1977

BRIAN CLARKE

Window in the Queen's Medical Centre, University of Nottingham, 1977
Architects: Building Design Partnership

"Dangerous Visions #1," acrylic on panel and
slashed canvas with jumbo clips and varnish,
1977 (4 ft. × 4 ft.)

BRIAN CLARKE

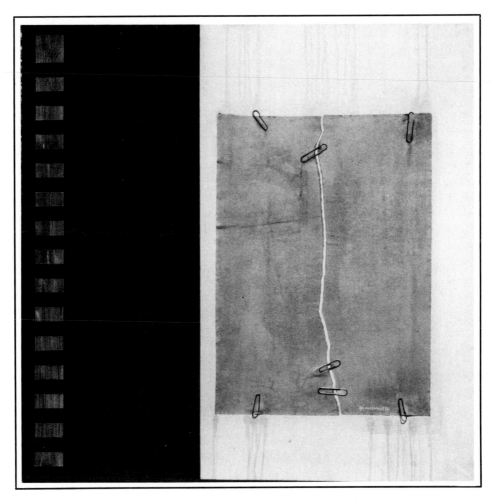

"Dangerous Visions #2," acrylic on panel with paper
and jumbo clips applied to canvas,
1977 (4 ft. × 4 ft.)

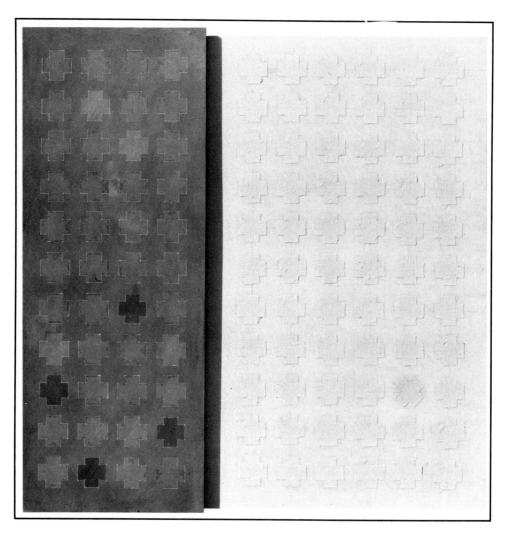

Acrylic on panel and canvas, 1978
(4 ft. × 4 ft.)

BRIAN CLARKE

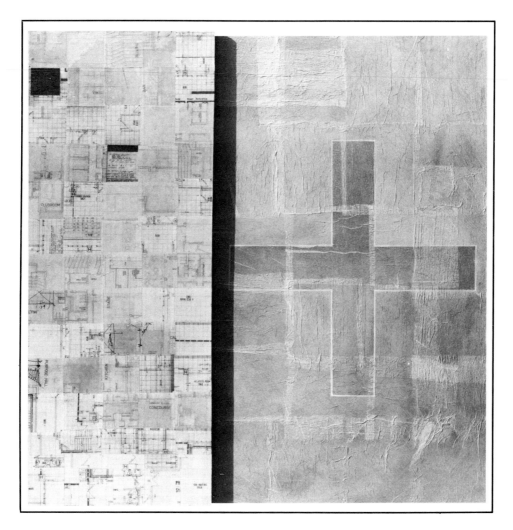

Acrylic on panel with varnished tissue and architectural plans, 1978
(4 ft. × 4 ft.)

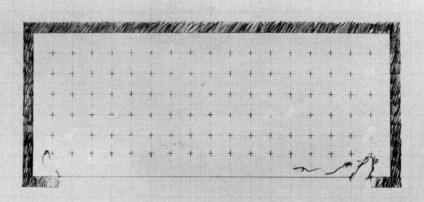

Drawing, 1978

BRIAN CLARKE

Painting in acrylics with reversed canvas stretcher entitled,
"Tribute to Kasimir Malevitch," 1977 (4 ft. × 4 ft.)

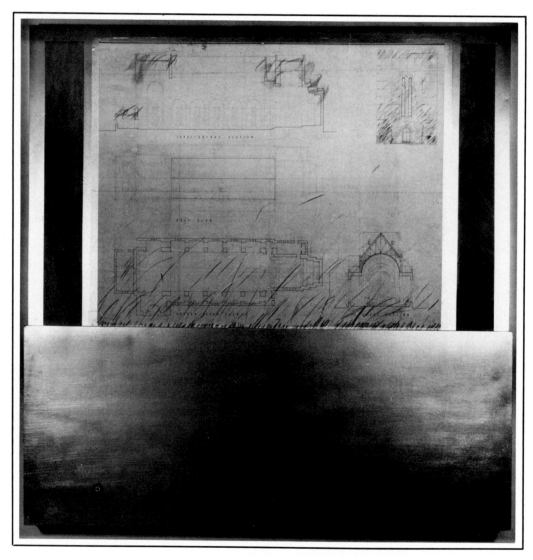

''Velarde Is Not Mocked.''
Architectural plan and chrome on panel, 1977 (4 ft. × 4 ft.)

John Piper, born in 1903 in Epsom, England, studied at the Richmond School of Art, Royal College of Art, and Slade School of Fine Art. In 1933, he visited Paris where contact with Brancusi, Braque, Helion, and Léger stimulated an experiment in 2D abstract compositions. In 1939, he and Myfanwy Evans edited the avant-garde quarterly, *AXIS*. During 1941 and 1942, he was commissioned by the Queen to paint a series of works based on Windsor Castle. During World War II, along with Henry Moore and Graham Sutherland he was made an official war artist. Under the influence of the more poetic forms of surrealism he turned, in the late '30s, to a romantic naturalism, returning to his earlier interests in architecture.

He has collaborated on many operas as designer with Benjamin Britten, and he has had many one-man exhibitions throughout the world, his work on display in most of the major collections, including The Tate Gallery, Victoria and Albert Museum, Contemporary Art Society, Museum of Modern Art New York, and so on. The author of *Wind in the Trees* (*Poems*) (1921), *Brighton Aquatints* (1935), and *Building and Prospects* (1949), Mr. Piper is currently represented in London by the Marlborough Gallery.

Selected projects include: 3-light East window, St. Giles' Totternhoe, Bedfordshire, 1970–71; St. George's Chapel, George VI Memorial Chapel, Windsor Castle, 1969; East window, St. Peter's Babraham, Cambridgeshire, 1966; Eight windows of Chapel, Churchill College, Cambridge, 1970; St. Andrew's, Plymouth, Devonshire, 1962–68; Metropolitan Cathedral of Christ the King, Liverpool, 1965–67; St. Margaret's, Westminster, London, 1967–68; Interior mural on staircase, Sanderson's Store, Berners Street, London, 1959–60; East End Rose window, St. Woolo's Cathedral, Newport, Monmouthshire, 1964; School Chapel, Oundle, Northamptonshire, 1954–56; West window, St. Mark's, Sheffield, Yorkshire, 1963–64; St. Mary's Church, Swansea, Wales 1965–66; 3-light East window high above Altar, Cathedral at Llandaff, Wales,

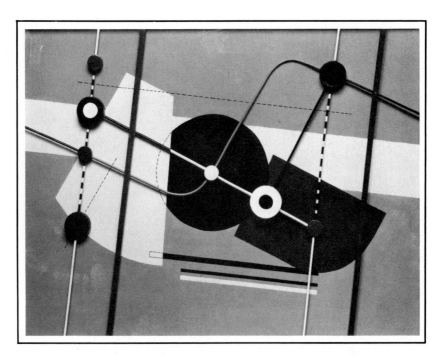

Constructivist Painting, 1934 (Tate Gallery collection)

Beach Object, 1937 (mixed media)

JOHN PIPER

Window in Eton College Chapel, 1958–61
Architect: Sir William Holford

Coventry Cathedral Baptistry Window,1959–62
Architect: Sir Basil Spence

176
JOHN PIPER

Painting, St. Léger, 1967
(Marlborough Fine Art Ltd)

JOHN PIPER

Preliminary design for the projected chapel window
Robinson College, Cambridge, England, 1978

JOHN PIPER

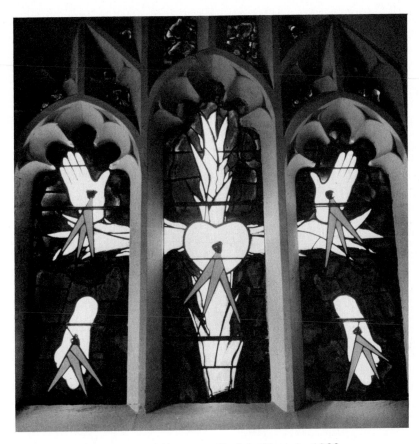

Window in Misterton Parish Church, 1966

Window in St. Andrew's Church, Wolverhampton, 1973–74
Architect: A. R. Twentyman

Overleaf: ''Garn Fawr,'' 1969, (gouache, 37.5 cm. × 54.5 cm.)
(Marlborough Fine Art Ltd)

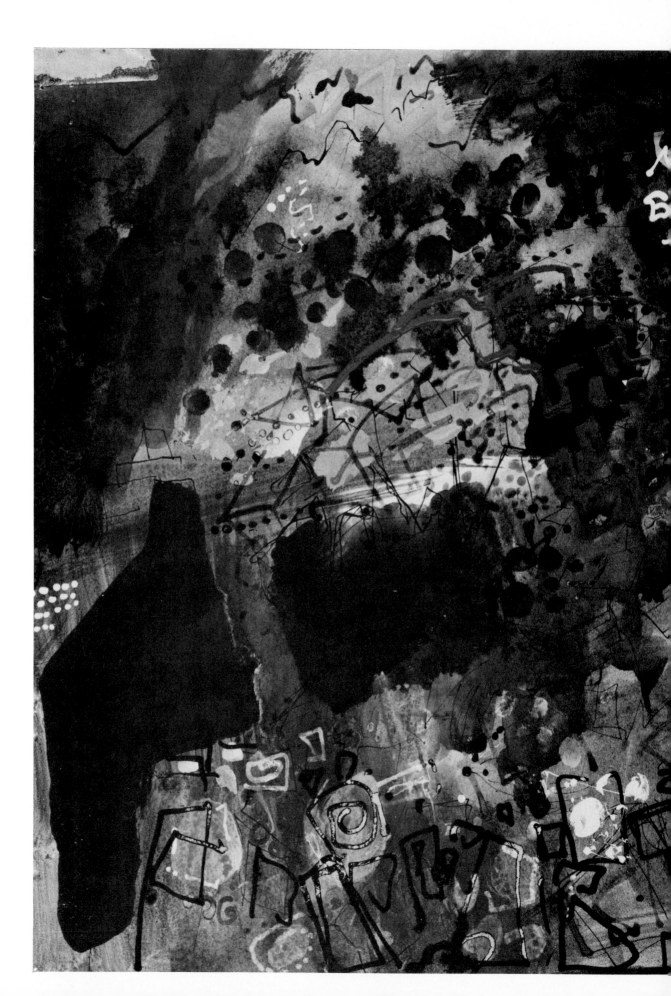

"Foliate Heads," 1953

Painting (gouache), 1970 (Marlborough Fine Art Ltd)

Ray Bradley

Ray Bradley was born in 1938 in Surrey and attended the Wimbledon School of Art from 1953–57; and the Royal College of Art from 1959–62; and has been working independently since then. He was awarded the Worshipful Company of Glaziers Award (Travelling Fellowship) in 1966, and C.A.C. Bursary in 1976.

His many projects include: St. Peter's, Thundersley, Essex, 1966; Hatchetts', Piccadilly, London, 1967; Post House Hotel, Hampstead, 1970; Park Lane, Penthouse, 1973; Bar Hill Church, Cambridge, 1974; Christ Church Orpington, 1976; and private residences in Dubai, Lagos, and Bahrain, 1978.

RAY BRADLEY

West Window, Christ Church, Orpington, Kent 1976

RAY BRADLEY

Baptistry Screen, etched and sandblasted, Bar Hill Church, Cambridge, 1974
Architects: John Pook and Gerald Smith

Triptych Windows, Penthouse, Park Lane, London, 1973

RAY BRADLEY

Glass Applique, Part of a Complex of Four Interior Screens,
Post House Hotel, Hampstead, London,1970

Stairway Window, Private House, Kensington, 1970

Patrick Reyntiens

ANDY EARL

Patrick Reyntiens was born in London in 1925 and educated at Ampleforth College, 1940–43; Marylebone School of Art, 1943–47; and Edinburgh School of Art, 1950–52; and studied stained glass under J. E. Nuttgens, 1952–54. He has collaborated on stained glass with John Piper, Ceri Richards, Brian Young and Philip Sutton. Mr. Reyntiens has had one-man shows of stained glass in Edinburgh, London, and Reading and much of his work is in private collections in England and the USA. He is the author of the definitive book on the craft of stained glass, *The Technique of Stained Glass,* and is currently a member on the advisory panel of Decoration to Westminster Cathedral and Brompton Oratory, of the Crafts Advisory Committee, and of the Court of the Royal College of Art.

His many projects include: Rose window, Christ Church, Flackwell Heath, Buckinghamshire, 1962; both nave ranges of windows, St. Mary's Nursing Home, Ednaston, Derbyshire, 1965; 3-light window in Chapel, Oratory Preparatory School, Branksome Park, Poole, Dorset, 1964; 2-light window, Clifton School Chapel, Bristol, Gloucestershire, 1964; 3-light window, St. Mary's, Hounds, Hampshire, 1962; west window (1968) and Lady Chapel window (1969) of All Saints, Odiham, Hants.; two east windows, Parish Church at Hinton Ampner, Hants., 1970; total glazing of Church in Dalle-de-Verre, St. Mary's Priory, Leyland, Lancashire, 1964–65; lantern, nave windows and some site Chapel windows Dalle-de-Verre, Metropolitan Cathedral of Christ the King, Liverpool, Lancashire, 1965–67; baptistery and east window, St. Margaret's, Twickenham, London, 1968–69; private Chapel, Oratory School, Fulham, London, 1970; private Chapel at No. 58, Holland Park, London, 1970; east window, St. Anselm's, Southall, London, 1971; four large decorative panel windows, Unicorn Building, Johannesburg, South Africa, 1968; and 3-light General White memorial window, Episcopalian Cathedral, Washington, DC, 1968–69.

Window in Baptistery, 1968–69 St. Margaret's Church, Twickenham,
Architects: Williams and Winkley

PATRICK REYNTIENS

Sanctuary window St. Margaret's Church, Twickenham

Above and right: Windows in private chapel in
the Oratory Secondary School, Fulham, London, 1970
Architects: David Stokes and Partners

PATRICK REYNTIENS

"Transfiguration," one of three free-standing windows in
the library of the Cowley Road
Church of England Secondary School, Oxfordshire, 1976

Peter Mollica

Peter Mollica was born in 1941 in Newton, Massachusetts and was educated at Northeastern University in Boston. From 1964 to 1968 he was apprenticed to Chris Rufo, also in Boston. Throughout his apprenticeship and later, he travelled and studied stained-glass windows in England, Denmark, France, and Germany, and in 1975 studied stained-glass design with Ludwig Schaffrath and Patrick Reyntiens in Loudwater, Buckinghamshire, England. He has numerous commissioned works all over California, as well as some in Nevada, New York, Massachusetts, Maine, Minnesota, Oklahoma, and Valais, Switzerland.

Publications by Peter Mollica include: *Stained Glass Primer,* vols. 1 and 2, 1971; "Schaffrath at Burleighfield House," *Stained Glass,* 1975; and "What's Happening to Stained Glass?", *Stained Glass,* 1976.

Stairway Window, Berkeley, California, 1975

PETER MOLLICA

Office Window, Marquis Associates, San Francisco, California, 1976

Tub Window, California, 1975

Residence Window, San Francisco, California, 1977

Residence Window, Kensington, California, 1977

Stairway Window, San Francisco, California, 1976

David Wilson

David Wilson was born in 1941 and grew up in North Yorkshire. From 1957 to 1961 he attended Middlesbrough College of Art Cleveland where he studied general arts and stained glass. During 1961 and 1962 he studied stained glass under Thomas Fairs at Central School of Arts and Crafts, London. From 1962 to 1971 Wilson worked as a designer for Rambusch Decorating Company in New York. After four years of working independently on various commissions, Wilson returned to Rambusch Associates for a short period working as the supervisor of the stained-glass department. He also designs commissions independently and teaches stained glass at the Brooklyn Museum Art School. He is currently living in New York State.

His many projects include: Little Sisters of the Assumption, New York, New York, 1965; St. Vincent and Sarah Fisher Home, Farmington, Michigan, 1966; St. Gabriel's Monastery, Brighton, Massachusetts, 1967; St. Bernards Church, Saranac Lake, New York, 1968; Paul VI Convent, Clifton, New Jersey, 1969; St. Thomas More, Manalapan, New Jersey, 1970; Our Lady of Perpetual Help, Atlanta, Georgia, 1973; Temple Hesed, Scranton, Pennsylvania, 1973; St. Thomas More, Cherry Hill, New Jersey, 1974; Church of the Epiphany, Houston, Texas, 1974; Temple Emanuel, Houston, Texas, 1975; Immaculate Conception Cathedral, Burlington, Vermont, 1976.

Window in Paul VI Convent, Clifton, New Jersey

Window in St. Gabriel's Monastery, Brighton, Massachusetts, 1967
Architects: Shields Associates

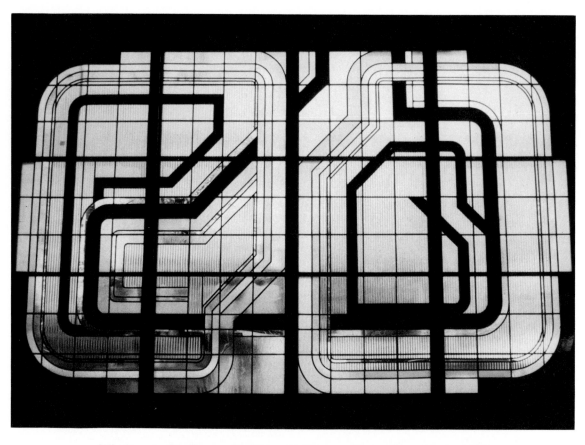

Window in St. Bernard's Church, Saranac Lake, New York, 1968
Architects: Finnegan, Lyon and Colburn

Window in St. James Church, Clarksburg, West Virginia, 1974
Architects: Wilson and King

Window in St. Thomas More Church,
Cherry Hill, New Jersey, 1974
Architects: Geddes Brecher, Qualls and Cunningham

Ed Carpenter

Ed Carpenter was born in 1946 in Los Angeles, California and attended the University of California, Santa Barbara, and Berkeley from 1965 to 1966 and from 1968 to 1970. From 1969 through 1975 he made a number of visits to glass factories, window installations, and stained-glass artists throughout Europe. In 1973 he studied stained glass design and technique with Patrick Reyntiens in Buckinghamshire, England. In 1975 Mr. Carpenter studied large architectural stained glass design with Ludwig Schaffrath in Alsdorf, West Germany and received the Michael Hattrell Award for the study of stained glass in modern architecture from Burleighfield Assoc., also in Buckinghamshire.

He has completed many projects throughout Oregon, California, Texas, Illinois, Louisiana, and Buckinghamshire, England, among them: Mono County Courthouse, Bridgeport, California, 1974; the Christ Episcopal Church, Lake Oswego, Oregon, 1974; Adventist Hospital Chapel, Portland, Oregon, 1976; St. Clare Catholic Church, Portland, Oregon, 1977; and to be completed by 1979, Oregon State Executive Office Building, Salem, Oregon.

Chapel Windows, Christ Church, Lake Oswego, Oregon, 1974

ED CARPENTER

Lobby View, Portland Adventist Hospital Glass and Door Design

ED CARPENTER

Window in Residence, Portland, Oregon, 1976

Window in Residence, Portland, Oregon, 1976

Window in the entry of Portland, Oregon Residence 1975
Architect and Landscape Designer: Richard Painter

Exterior view

ED CARPENTER

Window in Residence, Portland, Oregon
Architect: Carole Edelman, 1975

GLOSSARY

ARTS AND CRAFTS MOVEMENT
English social and aesthetic movement of the latter half of the nineteenth century, growing out of the widespread dissatisfaction with the quality of manufactured products, and moving towards a return to the "idyllic" character of the medieval tradition of craftsmanship. Ruskin was the major theorist of the movement, but it was William Morris and his group who turned the theory into practical activity.

AUTOMATIC ART or AUTOMATISM
Drawing without objective reference. The surrealists literally shut their eyes and drew. The subconscious expression manifested in line.

"DER BLAUE REITER"
A group of Munich artists to whom the title "The Blue Rider" was given in 1911 by its two most important members, Kandinsky and Marc. The name of the group derived from the title of one of Kandinsky's pictures. In 1912, Paul Klee and the French Cubists, notably Delaunay, also joined the group. It was certainly the most significant manifestation of abstract art in Germany before 1914, being less nationalistic and wider in scope than the earlier expressionist group, Die Brücke.

BRANDCOLLAGE
A specific type of collage developed by Johannes Schreiter in 1958, in which he uses burned and smoke-stained paper in his paintings and assemblages.

CLOISONNISME
A method of painting influenced by cloisonné enamels; strong, flat forms in bright colors with blue or blue-black contours separating the color area. The style was developed by Émile Bernard (1868–1941) after he had experimented with Signac's *pointillisme* in 1886 and had been influenced by his friend, Gauguin, later that year.

DE STIJL
One of the most influential of modern art movements originating in the journal De Stijl of 1917, founded by a small but closely-linked group of Dutch painters and architects. The leaders of the De Stijl group, or, as they are sometimes called, the neo-plasticists (the name taken from a pamphlet printed by the group in 1920) were the painter Piet Mondrian, the painter/architect Theo Van Doesburg, and the architect J.J.P. Oud. The school aimed towards the goal of relating all forms of visual art, particularly painting, sculpture, architecture, and industrial design. The steps toward rectilinear simplifications made by the group are most strikingly articulated in the paintings of Mondrian, whose work was a major influence on such important polemicists as Gropius and Le Corbusier.

NEW WAVE
In the context of this book, the term "new wave" refers specifically to the musical revolution that occurred in Britain in 1976, the initial stage of which was punk rock.

OMEGA WORKSHOP
Working on lines similar to those of the firm of William Morris, the Omega workshops, founded by Roger Fry in 1913, propogated the philosophy of bringing modern art into touch with daily domestic life by the production of decorative art. Believing that the artistic spirit should be channeled into the production of everyday objects, their number included Duncan Grant and Vanessa Bell. Omega closed in 1919.

VIENNESE SECESSION
Founded in 1897 by Gustav Klimt, the Secession was as much concerned with the applied arts and architecture as with painting. The exhibitions of this group and its periodical, *Ver Sacrum,* did much to spread Jugendstijl, the German variety of art noveau.

VORTICISM
A variety of cubism exclusive to England and led by Wyndham Lewis (1884–1957). The magazine, *Blast,* the literary organ of the

group, was edited by Lewis and aligned itself to European cubism and futurism. The first so-called vorticist work was painted by Lewis in 1912. Bomberg, Epstein, Etchells, Gaudier-Brzeska, Nevinson, Roberts, and Wadsworth were linked with the movement.

DEUTSCHER WERKBUND

An organization of German designers, architects, and manufacturers whose common aim was the improvement of design of machine-made products. Founded in 1907, its best-known members were Henri van de Velde, Peter Behrens, and Hermann Muthesius. In 1914, the Werkbund held a special exhibition of members' work in Cologne. This show introduced to the public the early work of Gropius and Taut, Gropius' model factory building being the most often discussed of the exhibits. Though the Werkbund became inactive for a number of years, it was revived soon after the Second World War.

NOTES

TOWARD A NEW CONSTRUCTIVISM, Brian Clarke

1. Herbert Read's introduction to *Paul Klee on Modern Art,* Faber and Faber, London, 1953.

2. Balilla Pratella, from *Manifesto of Futurist Musicians,* 1910/*Futurist Manifestos,* Umbro Apollonio, Ed., Thames and Hudson, London, 1973, p. 31.

3. Ada Louise Huxtable, *New York Times,* April 16, 1978.

4. Thomas Joshua Cooper's and Paul Hill's catalogue, *Remnants and Prenotations,* Arnolfini Gallery, Bristol, England, 1974. (Cooper, not Hill, belongs to the school of post-Weston photographers.)

5. Ralph Gibson, *The Somnambulist, Days at Sea, and Deja Vu,* 2/e, Lustrum Press, New York, 1973.

6. *Peter Getting out of Nicks Pool* (1965). Painting by David Hockney in the collection of the Walker Art Gallery, Liverpool, England. *David Hockney* by David Hockney, Thames and Hudson, London, 1976, no. 145.

7. For those who haven't burned it as she suggested, see Yoko Ono's letter to Ivan Karp of January 4th, 1965 reprinted in *Grapefruit,* by Simon and Schuster, New York, 1969.

8. See the *Blue Guitar* suite of etchings (20) published by Petersburg Press, London and New York, 1976.

9. The Metropolitan Opera House, Lincoln Center for the Performing Arts, New York, *Source of Music,* mural 30′ × 36′, 1966.

10. Pan American World Airways Building Inc., N.Y.; Architects—Emery Roth and Sons; Design Consultant—Walter Gropius (The Architects Collaborative, Inc.); Joseph Albers—plastic laminated mural, 60′ × 27′.

11. See *Calder* by Mulas and Arnason, Viking Press, New York, 1971.

12. Proclamation from the Weimar Bauhaus, 1919. See *Bauhaus 1919–28,* The Museum of Modern Art, New York, 1928.

13. Camilla Gray: *The Great Experiment: Russian Art 1863–1922,* Thames and Hudson, London, 1962.

14. Charles Jencks: *Modern Movements in Architecture,* Doubleday, Garden City, NY, and Penguin Books, Harmondsworth, 1973.

15. Harry Callahan, arguably the most significant photographer in America, spent his working life teaching. It is only now that photographers, even in America, can exist from the sales of their prints, and still very few are in this position.

16. See *The Essential Writings of Marcel Duchamp,* edited by Michael Sanouillet and Elmer Peterson, Thames and Hudson, London, 1975.

17. *Studio International,* July/August (1975) ''Photographic Practice and Art Theory,'' by Victor Burgin.

18. *Complexity and Contradiction in Architecture,* by Robert Venturi, rev. ed., New York Graphic Society, Greenwich, CT, 1977.

19. Charles Jencks: *Modern Movements in Architecture,* Doubleday, Garden City, NY, and Penguin Books, Harmondsworth, 1973.

20. Of course, this discounts the important work designed for historical buildings such as Poensgen's small window for the Alte Kappelle in Rhondorf or Schreiter's remarkable work for Heidelberg.

21. *Building Design,* (Piano and Rogers) ''Colour in Architecture,'' London, 9/30/77.

22. *Leger and Purist Paris,* John Golding and Christopher Green: Fernand Leger, The Tate Gallery for the exhibition of the same name, London, 1971.

23. Letter from Poensgen to Clarke, June, 1976.

24. Le Corbusier, *The History of the Window* (unpublished).

25. From letter to the author from D. A. Button, Dip. Arch., RIBA, of Pilkington Brothers Ltd., St. Helens, England.

26. Reyner Banham: *The Architecture of the Well Tempered Environment,* University of Chicago Press, Chicago, and Architectural Press, London, 1969.

27. Paul Scheerbart and Bruno Taut from Paul Scheerbart: *Glasarchitektur* (dedicated to Taut), reprinted by Praeger, New York, 1972.

A SHORT HISTORY OF THE DEVELOPMENT OF TWENTIETH-CENTURY GERMAN STAINED GLASS, M. Coulon-Rigaud

1. Hoelzel, tying in with Goethe's ideas, worked out a theory of color after 1905, which related a theory of regularities in musical harmony to color. His special claim to fame apart from that lies in the fact that as a member of the Dachau group, a circle of landscape painters, he made the step into abstract art even before Kandinsky. His pronounced experimental interest in the phenomenon of color led to the excess of color blends in the windows he produced in 1917 for the Bahlsen Works in Hannover. This is emphasized by his use of lead to bring several colors together.

2. Paul Wember demonstrates this development clearly in the catalogue, *Johan Thorn Prikker,* which was published in 1966 by Scherpe of Krefeld.

3. Important windows by Campendonk can be found in Essen-Münster (1952–53) in the crypt of Bonn-Münster (1931) and in the Gemeente Museum in The Hague (his Passion Window of 1937).

4. In addition to the well-known monumental windows in Aachen Cathedral (1951), I would also refer you to Wendling's earlier works in the Church of the Holy Ghost in Aachen (1930), and also to the windows in Xanten Cathedral (1963).

5. E.g., those in the Franciscan Monastery in Werl (1937).

6. See the monograph, *Ludwig Schaffrath,* Scherpe, Krefeld, 1977.

7. I would draw your attention to his windows in the Parish Church of Bad Kissingen (1958–60), the sixteen windows in the Church of St. Mary in Kalk (Cologne) (1965), the west rose window in the Church of Elisabeth in Marburg, and the passionate windows in the Protestant Church in Sobernheim (1962–64).

8. South window of St. Margaret's, Burgstadt/Main (1959–60).

9. For evidence, you should look at his impressive concrete and glass walls in St. Martin's, Bad Honnef (1967–68) or his leaded glass windows in Pilgerzell (1965).

10. The very condensed works of M. Klos in the Catholic Church of Donsbrüggen in the Lower Rhine region (1961), in the Church of the Assumption in Münchengladback (1967), and in St. Cyriakus, Weeze (1968) are certainly among the best windows he produced in leaded glass.

11. See the Cathedral cloisters in Aachen (1962–65), the Carmelite Monastery in Düren (1964), and St. Mary the Queen, Troisdorf (1961).

12. A striking example of such a freely patterned lead is the east-window frieze in the devotion room in Leutesdorf on the Rhine (1966).

13. More developed variants of this new type of window are to be found in St. Ansgar's in Södertälje, Sweden (1976–77), in St. Laurentius, Niederkalbach (1976–78), and in Limburg Cathedral (1976–77).

14. The east wall of the Church of the Holy Ghost in Dortmund (1970) offers quite an excellent expression and a genuine enrichment of op art.

THE RAW MATERIAL GLASS AS A LIGHT FILTER, Johannes Schreiter

1. Bernhard's mysticism excluded from the church environment anything which could distract from the practice of devotion, as this was deemed to bring about the experiencing of God in the human soul. He therefore recommended gray glass (*grisaille*) for the windows. This is characterized by chromatic shades of gray closely knitted together by a strictly linear wicker-work effect based on a series principle.

2. Hans H. Hofstätter: *Johannes Schreiter—"Recent Glass Images,"* Heinz Moos Verlag, Munich, 1965.

3. That applies, for example, to black and white painting which stood in contrast to the baroque informal style, or to minimal art.

4. See Herbert Schade, S. J.: "Information on the Theme of the Church and Art" in *The Spiritual Environment as the Church Council See It,* Verlag der Deutschen Gesellschaft für Christliche Kunst, Munich, 1969.

5. Susanne K. Langer: *Philosophy on a New Track,* S. Fischer, Frankfurt, 1965.

6. See Dietrich Helms: "The Case for White and Black, Monochrome Painting and Girke," *Egoist 7,* Verlag Adam Seide, Frankfurt, 1965.

7. Wassily Kandinsky: *On the Spiritual Nature of Art,* Benthely Verlag, Bern and Munich, 1912.

8. Rainer Volp: *Art as Symbol,* Gütersloher Verlagshaus Gerd Mohn, Gütersloh, 1966.

9. The use of light membranes in an architectural context are evidenced in the glass by W. Buschulte in the chancel of St. Dionysios, Essen-Barbeck (1964) and in the nave of St. Folian, Aachen (1962); by Jochem Poensgen in St. John the Baptist Church in Wuppertal-Oberbarmen (1967–68) and in the Chapel of Maria, Rhöndorf on the Rhine, containing beautiful silver-yellow brogues (1973); by Johannes Schreiter in St. Maria's, Göttingen (1969–70); and by Hubert Spierling in the Chancel of Maria Laach Abbey (1966).

10. We are indebted to Boris Kleint and Adolf Luther for their fundamental experiments; their marvelous white pictures between glass have unfortunately remained as movable objects, i.e., they haven't found a firm place in architecture. To create these pictures between glass factory scraps and glass objects—*trouvé's* were used aleatorically, or in set orders, which astonishingly, no one else has done or is doing. I know of only a couple of efforts by Josef Albers from his Bauhaus days, in which he put together bottle bottoms and other transparent rubbish in bright colored arrangements. (Illustration in Eugen Gomringer: *Josef Albers,* Josef Keller Verlag, Starnberg, 1971.)

11. Meistermann did some similar figurative windows, at least with the help of gray glass, some years later for St. Borromäus in the Sulz district of Cologne.

12. An exception to this are the spacious *grisailles* in the public part of the German Bank, Frankfurt, installed in 1971. Here the graphic flow is accompanied by fine contrasts in color tone, without losing the *grisaille* character.

13. A detailed account by Marcel Coulon-Rigaud appears in *Glasforum,* 2nd ed., Verlag Karl Hofmann, Schorndorf, 1973, p. 32 ff.

14. Illustrated in *Das Münster,* no. 1 (1969), pp. 4 ff.

15. See also the windows made of verdigris milk-glass with their bizarre, net-like liquefaction, in the ceiling construction of the Catholic Church in Pilgerzell by Jochem Poensgen (1965). Pictured in *Das Münster,* no. 3/4 (1966), pp. 106 ff.

16. Robert Sowers: *Stained Glass as an Architectural Art,* Zwemmer, London, 1961.

17. Pictured in *Das Münster,* no. 11/12 (1962), p. 434.

18. See Marcel Coulon-Rigaud: "Johannes Schreiter," *Glasforum,* no. 6 (1969), pp. 16 ff.

19. Robert Kudielka: "Art Technology," *Das Kunstwerk,* Oct./Nov. 1969.

20. See Wolfgang Schöne: *On Light in Painting,* Verlag Gebrüder Mann, Berlin, 1954, pp. 37 ff.

21. Also the tightly strung antique-glass tapestries by Vincenz Pieper in Paderborn Cathedral (1955), by W. Buschulte in the Parish Church of Linnich/Rhineland (1969), by Jochem Poensgen in St. Bonifatius, Lörrach, and by Ludwig Schaffrath in the Weekday Chapel of St. John, Merkstein (1974) are made from clear glass. They are a logical extension of the tradition of medieval ornamental pieces. (See Elmar Jansen: *A Short History of German Stained Glass,* VEB Verlag der Kunst, Dresden, 1963, pp. 16 ff.)

22. Illustrated in: *Das Münster,* 1963, no. 11/12, p. 424 ff and no. 5/6 (1969), p. 2121.

23. See Johannes Schreiter: "Concrete-Glass Windows," *Reports on Technical Glass,* Verlag der Deutschen Glastechnischen Gesellschaft, Frankfurt/Main, 1969. A year before Hajek, H. Lander achieved a no less impressive combination of concrete and clear glass in the Church of the 12 Apostles. (See *Art and The Church,* no. 2 (1969), pp. 55 ff.)

Jochem Poensgen's double-layered concrete ornamental mesh in the Catholic Church in Königsfeld/Black Forest (1971–72) is installed inside and out with an 85-meter-long wire ornamental glass image, in between in such a way that the outer concrete pillars appear as a soft silhouette in the geometrical pattern of the inner mesh. Pictured and described in *Das Münster,* no. 3 (1973), p. 156.

24. As shown by the *grisailles* by Joachim Klos in the Protestant Church of Wesel-Feldmark (1964); by W. Buschulte in St. Franziskus Holtheim (1965); by Johannes Schreiter in the Gothic Church of Mary, Göttingen, (1969–70)—made of concrete and glass (published in *Das Münster,* no. 2/3, (1971), pp. 136 ff.) and in the Protestant Church in Hofen/Black Forest (1974); by Jochem Poensgen in the Priest of Ars Church, Lintorf, near Düsseldorf (1965), also made of concrete and glass; (pictured in *Das Münster,* no. 3/4 (1966), p. 109 ff.); and last but not least, the extremely differentiated glass tapestries in the Gothic Chancel of the Church of the Pilgrims, Marienbaum near Xanten, by Erich Feld, made between 1964 and 1966.

25. Pictured in *Craft Horizons,* May/June 1969, p. 14.

26. Bernd Rosenheim had his wide-ranging and heavily leaded glass walls in the Chapel of Rest in Dietzenbach/Hessen (1967). (See *Glasforum,* no. 6 (1967), pp. 28 ff.)

27. Also to be seen in the white chancel windows of the Catholic Church of Aldenhoven (1964) by Schaffrath, in his white windows sparingly decorated with opal in St. Joseph's, Aachen (1965), in the St. Pius windows in the Zollstock district of Cologne (1963) by Buschulte, and in the "iridescent" *grisailles* made entirely from opal glass by the latter in St. Pius, Münster/Westfalia (1964).

28. Mention must be made here of the six white window walls by Schaffrath in the Catholic Church of Laasphe (1969).

29. Special mention is deserved by the simple "Dall-glass" windows by Buschulte in St. Clemens, Drolshagen (1966) (pictured in *Das Münster,* no. 1 (1969), p. 15); by Emil Kiess' glass *grisailles* in the Epiphany Church in Mannheim-Feudenheim (1963); by Markus Prachensky in the young people's room of the Catholic Church at Hasloch on the Main (1958) (pictured in *Das Münster,* no. 1/2 (1963), p. 32); and by Johannes Schreiter in St. Theresa's in Erlangen-Sieglitzhof (1972). My favorites are Schaffrath's prism windows in St. Bernhard's, Cloppenburg (1966–67) and St. Peter's in Merken. Further windows of this sort are situated in the Papst-Johannes House in Krefeld (1968), in the crypt of the Monastery at Bad Buchau (1966), and in the baptismal room of the Church of the Reconciliation in Bremen-Sebaldsbrück (1967). Ewald Mataré made the tower windows for Aachen town hall in 1962 out of various hollow-blown glass shapes which project outward.

30. Randomly made crystals of thick glass bring about a nervous, glowing effect. They assist in setting off certain shapes in W. Buschulte's windows in Niedermarsberg Hospital (1967). In most cases, however, such inclusions remain vulgar overdoses of a simple hash of light effects.

31. Pictured in *Das Münster,* no. 1/2 (1969), p. 6.

32. Pictured in *Das Münster,* no. 11/12 (1955), p. 356 ff.

33. Pictured in *Architectural Art and Work Form,* no. 3 (1957), p. 139.

34. Very impressive also is the shimmering of raw-material glasses with the famous "Herzogenrath" structure, as used by Emil Kiess in 1968 in his *grisailles* in Unter-türkheim, and the fine vibrating of the background section of clear "Listral" glass in Margarethe Keith's window wall in the Catholic Church of Heimbuchenthal/ Spessart (1972). (Depiction of a detail in *Das Münster,* no. 3 (1973), p. 159.)

35. See *Glasforum,* no. 4 (1965), p. 28 ff and *Das Münster,* no. 11/12 (1963), p. 386 ff.

36. Pictured in *Glasforum,* no. 6 (1967), p. 26 ff.

37. Pictured in *Saarheimat,* no. 1 (1965), p. 14 ff.

38. The thoughts of Ulrich Conrad on the crisis of sacred architecture in *Buildings for the Congregation of Tomorrow,* published by Hartmut Johnsen, Hamburg, 1969, go deeper into the problem I have alluded to here.

GOOD BEHAVIOR AND BAD TASTE, Patrick Reyntiens

1. If examples of official art are wanted, the most obvious might be the art of por-traiture.

2. We can instance *The Image in Search of Itself* by Victor Pasmore.

3. John Betjeman, *ARK,* Royal College of Art Journal, London, 1959.

4. Such a dislike of anything that is not plain and direct persists to this day in the interiors of chapels, however lavishly appointed the private homes of the congre-gation may be. Perhaps more than a hint of Manicheanism hovers around still.

5. Frances Yates, *The Art of Memory,* Routledge & Kegan Paul, London, 1966.

6. There is a correspondence between the integrity of the psyche's *interior* and the outward resulting work as a proof of its activity in individual Christian philosophy (principally St. Thomas Aquinas), which is echoed in the alchemical saying "as above, so below." That is, interiority and exterior tangible phenomena must pro-ceed to be modified in harmony, which is also the personal basis, in part, of modern art. There is also an interesting correspondence between the whole mental climate of the Bretheren of the Free Spirit in the thirteenth century and certain aspects of twentieth-century art. Indisputedly, certain attitudes of modern poetry from Rimbaud to Yeats and of authors such as James Joyce exhibit marked antinomian tendencies. There is also a parallel in the activities of the various antinomian sects and movements in present-day American, Japanese, and Ger-man society to similar activities in the Middle Ages. (See Norman Cohn, *The Pur-suit of the Millennium,* Paladin Books, London, 1964.)

7. The greatest problem, culturally speaking, for the twentieth and twenty-first cen-turies lies in the reconciliation—if it is possible—of the "organic" memory with the "inorganic," or reconstituted, memory of man. By the reconstituted memory is meant a memorative structure which is largely peripheral to the main motiva-tions of living. This could be shortened to the "museum" memory, because it is an undoubted fact that the displacement of artifacts from their intended environ-ment destroys a large proportion not only of their *significance,* but their very *memorative* and *associational envelope* in the interest of "pure, formal values" and aesthetic appreciation. Particularly obvious in the case of ethnic exhibits, it is sadly destructive of religious art (e.g., Italian quattrocento altar pieces stuffed into museums) and social art (e.g., frescoes taken from their *in situ* positions), and even of easel pictures, when museum presentation is taken as the norm from which all other presentation possibilities depart. Increasingly, sadly, this last is gaining ground in England.

8. The consequences of so frivolous and pragmatic an approach to the memorative processes is vividly and intelligently put forward by Susan Sontag in her introduction to *Cuban Revolutionary Posters*, Academy Books, London, 1972.

The Church remains today the easiest example to recognize of visual "organic memory" just as the museum is now, consciously, the shining example of "inorganic memory."

It is interesting to note that Mayr, the hitherto neglected master of Donizetti, writing as early as 1810, is quoted as saying: "I am certainly not with those who pretend that art must be only priestly and Catholic. Today art is free, independent and vital—religious persecution has been abolished. This does not mean, however, that we are unable to restate the origin with dignity. Modern art is founded in Catholicism, and has grown up in the Sanctuary amongst the fragrance of incense and the sound of hymns. The adolescent, when placed amidst the bustle of society, retains a trace which cannot be cancelled for it has been stamped on his brow by the sacred finger of priesthood. Today he is free and he has a tribute of homage to offer to the Catholic Church; and his mother must in turn drink to him a toast of goodwill. To follow any other cult would be a sign of ingratitude, sacrilege. In fact it is impossible to imagine that art forgets the Church which has so long nourished him, even in the hours of privation and misery: he cannot forget this in favor of Protestantism, who is like a woman who in the prime of life was incapable of a drop of milk from her stony breasts."

This implicitly distinguishes between the organic nature of the Catholic tradition and the pragmatic nature of the Protestant at that time. The appeal to scriptural authority of the sixteenth century may well be, in fact, the first instance of the museumistic state of mind—the *archaeological* approach, which ultimately denies the tradition of life.

9. One only has to instance the relationship of Cardinal Billot and Charles Maurras in early twentieth-century France to see how dangerous such a liaison can be from the Church's point of view. More often than not, the Church's interest in memory processes runs parallel to the secular interest, although, as recently in Francoist Spain, the two may appear all but identical over a certain time period. Of course the dictatorships of the left have made use of such techniques as well. Communism is certainly not free of the charge of using memory patterns in a manipulative way for the purposes of power.

10. We should not like to imply that all Jewish intelligentsia and revolutionaries were orthodox and practicing—far from it—but inculcated mental habits and patterns of thought persist even when overt allegiance to the faith has been surrendered. Thus, it is perfectly possible from a psychological point of view, if not a spiritual one, to remain Jewish or Catholic or Protestant in fundamental outlook while professing scepticism or atheism.

AUTONOMY AS A SPURIOUS ABSOLUTE, Robert Sowers

1. Barbara Rose (ed.), *Art as Art: The Selective Writings of Ad Reinhardt,* The Viking Press, New York 1975.

2. Robert Sowers, *Stained Glass and Architectural Art,* Zwemmer, London, 1961.

ART OR ANTI ART, John Piper

1. Robert Sowers: *Stained Glass, The Lost Art,* Lund Humphries, London, 1954.

2. J. Piper: *Stained Glass: Art or Anti-Art,* Studio Vista, London, 1968.

TWENTIETH-CENTURY STAINED GLASS, Martin Harrison

1. Herbert Read: *English Stained Glass,* G. P. Putnam & Son, London and New York, 1926, p. 226.

2. Pfaff, Konrad, *Ludwig Schaffrath: Stained Glass & Mosaic,* Scherpe Verlag Krefeld, 1977.

BIBLIOGRAPHY

STAINED GLASS

Amaya, M.: "The Taste of Tiffany," *Apollo Magazine,* February 1965, pp. 102–109.

Amaya, Mario: *Tiffany Glass,* Walker, New York, 1967.

Aubert, M.: *French Cathedral Windows of the 12th and 13th Centuries,* Iris Books, Oxford University Press, Oxford, 1947.

Beyer, V.: *Stained Glass Windows,* Oliver and Boyd, London, 1964.

Chagall, Marc: *The Jerusalem Windows,* New York Arts, New York, 1962.

Engels, M.T.: *Heinrich Campendock,* E.A. Seaman, Cologne, 1956.

Harrison, M. and B. Walters: *Burne-Jones,* Barrie and Jenkins, London, 1974.

Hofstatter, H.A.: *Johannes Schreiter Neue Glasbilder,* Heinz Moos Verlag, Munich, 1965.

Kerkramen, F.: *Vitraux de France,* Rijksmuseum, Amsterdam, 1973–1974.

Korn, A.: *Glass in Modern Architecture of the Bauhaus Period,* George Braziller, New York, 1968.

Lee, L.: *The Appreciation of Stained Glass,* Oxford University Press, London, 1977.

Lee, L., G. Seddon and F. Stephens: *Stained Glass,* Mitchell Beazley, London, 1977.

Marchini, G.: *Italian Stained Glass Windows,* Thames and Hudson, London, 1956.

McGrath, R. and A.C. Frodt: *Glass in Architecture and Decoration,* Architectural Press, London, 1961.

Mollica, P.: *Stained Glass Primer,* vol. 1, Mollica Stained Glass Press, Berkeley, CA, 1971.

Mollica, P.: *Stained Glass Primer,* vol. 2, Mollica Stained Glass Press, Berkeley, CA, 1971.

Mostyn, Lewis: *Stained Glass in North Wales Up to 1850,* John Sherratt and Son, Cheshire, 1970.

Musée des Arts Décoratifs des Paris, *Le Vitrail Français,* Éditions des Deux Mondes, Paris, 1968.

Newton, R.G.: *The Deterioration and Conservation of Painted Glass,* Oxford University Press, Oxford, 1974.

Piper, J.: *Stained Glass: Art or Anti-Art,* Studio Vista, London, 1968.

Rigan, O.B.: *New Glass,* San Francisco Book Company, San Francisco, 1976.

Reyntiens, P.: *The Technique of Stained Glass,* Watson-Guptill, New York, 1967.

Schaffrath, L.: *Stained Glass + Mosaic,* Scherpe Verlag, Krefeld, 1977.

Schneider, J.: *Glasgemalde,* Katalog der Sammlung des Schweizerischen Landesmuseums, vol. 1 Zurich, 1970.

Schneider, J.: *Glasgemalde,* Katalog der Sammlung des Schweizerischen Landesmuseums, vol. 2, Zurich, 1970.

Sewter, Charles A.: *The Stained Glass of William Morris and His Circle,* Yale University Press, New Haven, 1974.

Wember, P.: *Johan Thorn Prikker, Glasfenster, Wandbilder, Ornamente 1891–1932,* Sherpe Verlag, Krefeld, 1966.

Westlake, N.H.J.: *A History of Painted Glass,* 4 vols., James Parker, London, 1881.

Woodforde, C.: *English Stained Glass and Painted Glass,* Oxford University Press, Oxford, 1954.

van Beunigen, C.: *Stained Glass Windows,* Academy Editions, London, 1972.

ARCHITECTURE

Ambasz, E.: *The Architecture of Luis Barragán,* The Museum of Modern Art, New York, 1976.

Banham, R.: *The Architecture of the Well-Tempered Environment,* University of Chicago Press, Chicago, 1969.

Bauhaus, Royal Academy of Arts, London, 1968.

Bayer, H., W. Gropius and I. Gropius: *Bauhaus,* The Museum of Modern Art, New York, 1938.

Bertram, Anthony: *Design,* Penguin, New York and London, 1938.

Besset, M.: *Le Corbusier,* Rizzoli International, New York, 1976.

Blaser, W.: *Mies van der Rohe: The Art of Structure,* Praeger, New York, 1965.

Boyd, R.: *New Directions in Japanese Architecture,* George Braziller, New York, 1968.

Bullrich, F.: *New Directions in Latin American Architecture,* George Braziller, New York, 1969.

Cassou, J. and J. Leymarie: *Fernand Léger: Drawings and Gouaches,* New York Graphic Society, Greenwich, CT, 1973.

Dixon, R. and S. Muthesius: *Victorian Architecture,* Thames and Hudson, London, 1978.

Feuerstein, G.: *New Directions in German Architecture,* George Braziller, New York, 1968.

Gebhard, D.: *Schindler,* Thames and Hudson, London, 1971.

Gregotti, V.: *New Directions in Italian Architecture,* George Braziller, New York, 1968.

Hitchcock, Henry-Russell and Philip Johnson: *The International Style,* Norton, New York, 1966.

Hutton, G. and E. Smith: *English Parish Churches,* Reader's Union, Thames and Hudson, London, 1953.

James Stirling, Bauten und Projekte 1950–1974, Verlag Gerd Hatje, Stuttgart, 1975.

Jencks, C.: *The Language of Post-Modern Architecture,* Rizzoli International, New York, and Academy Editions, London, 1977.

Jencks, C.: *Modern Movements in Architecture,* Doubleday, Garden City, NY, 1973.

Jordon, R. F.: *Victorian Architecture,* Penguin, New York and London, 1966.

Josef Hoffman, 1870–1965: Architect and Designer, Fischer Fine Art Ltd., London, 1977.

Landau, R.: *New Directions in British Architecture,* George Braziller, New York, 1968.

Lasdun, D.: *A Language and a Theme: The Architecture of Denys Lasdun and Partners,* Riba, London, 1976.

Le Corbusier: *Towards a New Architecture,* Praeger, New York, 1970.

Mumford, L.: *Architecture as a Home for Man,* McGraw-Hill, New York, 1975.

Pevsner, N.: *Pioneers of Modern Design,* Pelican, New York, 1961.

Redstone, L.: *Art in Architecture,* McGraw-Hill, New York, 1968.

Richards, J.M.: *An Introduction to Modern Architecture,* Pelican, New York, 1940.

Robinson, C. and R.H. Bletter: *Skyscraper Style: Art Deco New York,* Oxford University Press, Oxford, 1975.

Rotzler, Willy: *Constructive Concepts,* A.B.C. Editions, Zurich, 1977.

Sharpe, D., ed: Scheerbart, P.; *Glass Architecture,* and Taut, B.; *Alpine Architecture,* November Books, London, 1972.

Venturi, R.: *Complexity and Contradiction in Architecture,* rev. ed., New York Graphic Society, Greenwich, CT, 1977.

Wagner, W.F.: *Houses Architects Design for Themselves,* McGraw-Hill, New York, 1974.

Wright, O.L.: *Frank Lloyd Wright,* Horizon, New York, 1976.

Wright, F.L.: *The Future of Architecture,* Horizon, New York, 1953.

Wright, F.L.: *In the Cause of Architecture,* ed. by Frederick Gutheim, McGraw-Hill, New York, 1975.

ART

Akademie-Sezession-Avantgarde um 1900, Kunsthalle, Darmstadt, 1966.

Apollonio, Umbro, ed.: *Futurist Manifestos,* Thames & Hudson, London, 1973.

Banham, R.: *Theory and Design in the First Machine Age,* 2nd. ed., Praeger, New York, 1967.

Barilli, R.: *Art Nouveau,* transl. by Raymond Rudorff, Paul Hamlyn, London, 1969.

Barker, P.: *Arts in Society,* Fontana/Collins, London, 1977.

Barnett Newman, Tate Gallery, London, 1972.

Battcock, G.: *The New Art: A Critical Anthology,* rev. ed., Dutton, New York, 1973.

Betjeman, J.: *John Piper,* Penguin, London and New York, 1944.

Bojko, Szymon: *New Graphic Design in Revolutionary Russia,* Praeger, New York, 1972.

Contemporanea, Incontri Internazionale d'Arte, Centro Di, Florence, 1973.

Crichton, M.: *Jasper Johns,* Harry Abrams, New York, 1977.

Die Abstrakten Hanover, Galerie Bargera, Cologne, 1975.

Die Buchkunst der Darmstädter Künstlerkolonie, Hessisches Landesmuseum, Darmstadt, Mathildenhöhe, 1976.

Die Künstler der Mathildenhöhe, Hessisches Landesmuseum, Darmstadt, Mathildenhöhe, 1976.

Die Stadt der Künstlerkolonie, Darmstadt 1900–1914, Hessisches Landesmuseum, Darmstadt, Mathildenhöhe, 1976.

Dine, Jim: *Jim Dine Prints 1970–1977,* Harper & Row, New York, 1977.

BIBLIOGRAPHY

Drawings by Kenneth Martin—Chance and Order, Waddington, London, 1973.

Duchamp, M.: *The Essential Writings of Marcel Duchamp,* ed. by Michel Sanouillet and Elmer Peterson, Thames and Hudson, London, 1975.

Ein Dokument Deutscher Kunst 1901–1976, Hessisches Landesmuseum, Kunsthalle, Darmstadt, Mathildenhöhe, 1976.

Gibson, Ralph: *Day at Sea: Forbidden Photographs,* Lustrum Press, New York, 1974.

Gibson, Ralph: *The Somnambulist,* 2nd ed., Lustrum Press, New York, 1973.

Golding, J. and C. Green: *Léger and Purist Paris,* Barron, 1977.

Gombrich, E.H.: *Norm and Form, Studies in the Art of the Renaissance,* Dutton, New York, 1971.

Gombrich, E.H.: *The Story of Art,* 12th ed., Dutton, New York, 1974.

Goosen, E.C.: *Ellsworth Kelley,* The Museum of Modern Art, New York, 1973.

Gregory, R.L. and E.H. Gombrich: *Illusion in Nature and Art,* Scribner, New York, 1974.

Groh, K.: *If I Had a Mind,* Verlag M. Dumont, Schaumberg, 1971.

Hayward Annual, 1977, Arts Council of Great Britain, London, 1977.

Herbin, Auguste and Ettienne Beothy: *Abstraction —Creation,* Cologne, 1974.

Hillier, B.: *The Austerity Binge,* Studio Vista, London, 1975.

Hockney, David: *David Hockney,* Thames and Hudson, London, 1976.

Hockney, David: *72 Drawings,* Jonathon Cape, London, 1971.

Yves Klein 1928–1962 Selected Writings, Tate Gallery, London, 1974.

Johannes Schreiter, Das Graphische Werk 1966–1977, Stadtische Galerie, Wolfsburg, 1978.

Julius Bissier, Kunstammlung Nordrhein-Westfalen, Düsseldorf, 1970.

Julius Bissier 1893–1965, Arts Council of Great Britain, London, 1977.

Kinetics, Hayward Gallery, London, 1970.

Klee, P.: *Paul Klee on Modern Art,* Faber and Faber, London, 1953.

Klee, P.: *Pedagogical Sketchbook,* Praeger, New York, 1960.

Kunstlerkolonie Mathildenhöhe, 1899–1914, Hessisches Landesmuseum, Darmstadt, Mathildenhöhe, 1976.

Kunst und Dekoration 1851–1914, Hessisches Landesmuseum, Darmstadt, Mathildenhöhe, 1976.

Kurt Schwitters 1887–1948, Wallraf-Ritchartz Museum, Cologne, 1963.

Léger, F.: *Functions of Painting,* Thames and Hudson, London, 1973.

Lipman, J.: *Calder's Universe,* Thames and Hudson, London, 1977.

Lucie-Smith, E. and P. White: *Art in Britain 1969–1970,* J.M. Dent and Sons, London, 1970.

Malevich, Essays on Art 1928–1933, Borgen, Copenhagen, 1968.

Malevich and His Circle, intro. by J. Bowlt, Rosa Esman Gallery, New York, 1978.

Max Bill, Buffalo Fine Arts Academy, Buffalo, 1974.

Michel, M. and Robert Michel: *Ella Bergmann,* Galerie Bargera, Cologne, 1974.

Newton, E.: *European Painting and Sculpture,* Penguin, London and New York, 1941.

The Non-Objective World Twenty-Five Years 1914–1939, Anneley Juda Fine Art, London, 1977.

Pfaff, Konrad: *Ludwig Schaffrath: Stained Glass and Mosaic,* Scherpe Verlag, Krefeld, 1977.

Read, H.: *The Meaning of Art,* Praeger, New York, 1972.

Rolt, L.T.C.: *Isambard Kingdom Brunel,* Pelican, New York, 1970.

Schmalenbach, W.: *Chagall,* Uffici Press, Milan, 1956.

7e Biennale de Paris, Centro Di, Florence, 1971.

Smith, R.: *Seven Exhibitions 1961–1975,* Tate Gallery, London, 1974.

Szarkowski, John: *Callahan,* Aperture, Milltown, NY, 1976.

Tisdall, C. and A. Bozzolla: *Futurism,* Thames and Hudson, London, 1977.

Wilkinson, A.G.: *The Drawings of Henry Moore,* Tate Gallery, London, 1977.

INDEX